Acknowledgements

An English Country Cottage by James Matthews
City Hall Gallery, Chester, Fine Art Photograph Library

A Cottage Garden by James Matthews
Church Street Gallery, Fine Art Photograph Library

The Garden Path by James Matthews
City Hall Gallery, Chester, Fine Art Photograph Library

At Cocking, Sussex by James Matthews
Harper Fine Art, Fine Art Photograph Library

A Wayside Cottage by Helen Allingham (1848-1926)
Haynes Fine Art, Fine Art Photograph Library

A Picturesque Cottage Garden by Arther Claude Strachan (1865-1954)
Anthony Mitchell Fine Paintings, Fine Art Photograph Library

Anne Hathaway's Cottage by Arther Claude Strachan (1865-1954)
Haynes Fine Art, Fine Art Photograph Library

In The Cottage Garden, Alveston, Warwick by Arther Claude Strachan (1865-1954)
Gavin Graham Gallery, Fine Art Photograph Library

A Treasury of

Country
Cottages

DAILY JOURNAL

This edition exclusive to

(949) 587-9207
Text and Illustrations
© **ROBERT FREDERICKS LTD**

Journal

Journal

Journal

Journal

JAMES MATTHEWS.

Journal

Journal

JAMES MATTHEWS.

Journal

Journal

Journal

Journal

Journal

Journal

Journal

Journal

Journal

Journal

Journal

Journal

Journal

Journal

Journal

Friendship

Journal

Friendship

Journal

Journal

Journal

Journal

Journal

Journal

Journal

Journal

Journal

Journal

Journal

Journal

at Slinfold
Sussex

Journal

Journal

Journal

Journal

Journal

To one I love.

Journal

Journal

Journal

Journal

Journal

Journal

Journal

Journal

Journal

Journal

Journal

Journal

Journal

Journal

JAMES MATTHEWS

Journal

Journal

at Seddlesco

Journal

Journal

Journal

Journal

Journal

Journal

Journal

....
....
....
....
....
....
....
....
....
....
....
....
....
....
....
....
....
....
....
....
....
....
....
....
....

Journal

Journal

Journal

Journal

Journal

A Guide to Bible and Life

VOLUME 10

Study to shew thyself approved
unto God,
a workman that needeth not
to be ashamed,
rightly dividing the word of truth.

II TIMOTHY 2:15

FAMILY
BIBLE
LIBRARY

V. Gilbert Beers, Ph.D.,Th.D.

THE SOUTHWESTERN COMPANY

Nashville, Tennessee

What's in this volume

Copyright © 1971 by THE SOUTHWESTERN COMPANY, Nashville, Tennessee
Library of Congress Catalog Card No. 71-155623
Printed in the United States of America
R.R.D. 3-72

4

A Guide

---

to Parents

A Guide to Parents

For Such a Time As This

THE LAND in which Queen Esther lived was passing through troubled times. Power had fallen into the wrong hands and it was misused. Mischief was coming from high places. The evil Haman had laid plans to destroy the entire Jewish race, and unknown to him, Queen Esther would be destroyed with it.

But the Queen's cousin, Mordecai, sent a challenge to her. Only she could stop this mad scheme. But she must do it at the risk of her own life. In his challenge, Mordecai said, "Who knows whether you are come to the kingdom for such a time as this" (Esther 4:14).

The wise Mordecai knew that troubled times demand courageous action. It was true in Queen Esther's troubled times. It is true in our troubled times also.

As parents today we must accept Mordecai's challenge. A generation is threatened and we must do something about it. We cannot stand idly by and see our own children destroyed by the forces which press upon them from all sides.

If you are sometimes frightened by what you read in the newspapers, you are not alone. Millions of concerned parents are more frightened than they have ever been before. They have every reason to be frightened, too, for there are many destructive forces at work.

There are forces at work today which would destroy our nation. This frightens us. There are other forces which would endanger our homes and communities. This frightens us. And there are forces at work which would cause people to destroy themselves. This is perhaps the most frightening of all, for when we destroy ourselves, we become our own enemy.

A later chapter will discuss some of these self-destructive forces. Alcohol and tobacco were two of our most destructive forces until the past few years. Now a new cancer has come on the scene—the misuse of drugs. Each year, many young people die or are permanently injured because of their misuse of drugs. These forces cannot be ignored by Christian parents. A positive plan of action must be undertaken in each home, so

6

that the parent will be informed, and will inform his children, of the dangers of these destructive forces.

Never before in the history of the world has a generation of young people had so much potential to do good . . . or evil. Never has any generation had so much power. Young people today have the power to learn more than ever before, to develop skills which were beyond the reach of their predecessors, and to exert influence greater than that of any previous generation.

Young people today have more earning power than their predecessors, more spending power, and thus more power in shaping the decisions of manufacturers and advertisers. They have a greater voice in national affairs than ever before, a greater opportunity to travel, greater power in their cars, a greater voice in their careers.

With all this power, a new generation can shape the world. Tomorrow's leaders can destroy the world or call the world to repentance.

TOMORROW'S LEADERS IN TRAINING TODAY

The course of action of tomorrow's leaders depends on the training of today's children. The destiny of tomorrow's world, and those who will shape it, lies in the hands of today's parents. You, the parents of today's children, determine the course taken by tomorrow's leaders, for they are the children growing up in your homes right now.

A future president, senator, governor, minister, or evangelist may be playing in your backyard sandbox right now! Or could it be a future criminal? What a tragedy that would be!

TOMORROW'S TRAGEDIES CAN BE PREVENTED

Every gangster, dope pusher, thief, or prostitute of tomorrow is an innocent little child today, trusting someone to show him the Way of Life. Every one of these tragic persons of today was a little child of yesterday. But somone failed him. Someone was too busy to tell him about Jesus Christ. Someone was too involved in other things to share in his life.

This same tragedy repeats itself generation after generation. But it doesn't need to. If each parent would accept his responsibility as a parent, how different the world would become. If each Christian parent would guide his children into a happy life in Jesus Christ, how different our homes, churches, communities, and nation would become! This is our challenge to you, parent . . . for such a time as this!

What Can Parents Do?

THE MOST IMPORTANT JOB in the world is that of a parent. The parent is appointed by God to be a special caretaker over His creation, the child, for about eighteen years.

What happens to that child the rest of his life is shaped largely by what happens during those eighteen important years. Here are some specific steps a parent can take in shaping his child's life.

1. Set Your Own Life in Order

If your life is deficient, your child will be disappointed. The complete life is one built on Jesus Christ.

Make sure you have accepted Christ into your life and that you are following in His steps. If you walk in His ways, you will set a pattern worthy for your child to imitate.

2. Live What You Teach

The idea "don't do as I do, do as I say" is not acceptable to today's child. He wants to be like his heroes, and he wants his parents to be two of his most important heroes. One of the best lessons your child will learn is the one you live before him.

3. Keep in Touch

It is not enough to live in the same house with your child. You must involve yourself in his life.

Rapport begins the day your child is born. If you let the TV set keep your child entertained all day while you involve yourself in other things, how can you expect to communicate with him? If you give your child your money instead of your time, he will learn to despise both. Your child wants YOU.

4. Introduce Him to Christ

The most rewarding hours are those spent with the children in family Bible study and devotions. Through these hours, your child will learn to see Christ in you.

He will learn habits of Bible study and prayer which will last a lifetime. He will see his own need of Christ in his life. In these wonderful hours you can introduce your child to Christ and help him accept Him as Savior and Lord and begin a life as His disciple.

8

A Guide

---

to Growth

A Guide to Growth

Know Your Child

MUCH IS SAID TODAY of the generation gap. The teen-ager complains, "You just don't understand me." His parent grumbles, "Nobody can understand you."

The trouble in many homes is that neither teen-ager nor parent understands the other. In too many cases, neither is even trying to understand.

The Generation Gap

If an undesirable generation gap exists between parent and child, it is often like a deep canyon which parent or child thinks cannot be crossed. But there are two simple bridges which can cross this canyon and they are easy to build. But they do require building! One bridge is love. The other is understanding.

But the burden of bridge building lies first of all with the parent. It is the parent who has brought the child into the world and has led him since he was a baby. It is the parent who has been commissioned by God to shape the destiny of the child, not the reverse. Don't expect your child to start the bridge building first.

Bridge Building Starts at Birth

The time to start bridge building is the day your child is born. How much better if you can build a little bridge before the gap gets big. If you keep this gap bridged all through childhood, it will not be a problem when the teen years come.

Some ask, "Why don't we try to close the generation gap?" The answer is simple. You can't, and even if you could, you shouldn't. Imagine a parent who would think, talk, and behave like a teen! Or a teen who would think, talk, and behave like his parent. The gap places you, the parent, on a higher level of leadership. It gives the teen someone to look up to, a very important part of the teen years.

10

GROWTH—A PATH WITH MANY STEPPING STONES

Life consists of growth, from birth until death. Nobody stands still. The cells of our bodies are constantly replacing themselves. Our minds are always reaching out for something new to learn. Our hands must find some new activity to do each day. To stand still is to fall behind, for all others about us move ahead.

Growth touches many stepping stones through life. We are concerned in this section with the growth of a child, from the youngest years until he leaves home.

We want to understand how he thinks and how he behaves at each of these stepping stones. When we understand the child, we will understand how to live with him and work with him.

THE GOLDEN GOAL—SUCCESS

Every parent wants to see his child succeed. No good parent really wishes that his child would fail. To help your child fail, you need to do nothing. Just watch him grow up, and remain uninvolved.

But to help your child succeed requires some effort. It requires you. You, the parent, must constantly be involved in helping to shape your child's future. He can't do the job alone. It is too big. He needs you to help him.

Success may mean different things to different people. To some, success means nothing more than getting a good job with a large paycheck. To others, it means more, to make a worthwhile contribution in life. But to people who care about life's most important values, the golden goal of success means something far more. Here are three of the most important parts of success:

1. To know what we are and what we can become and to develop ourselves to the fullest.
2. To know God and what He can do for us and through us and to let Him work in us to the fullest.
3. To know our world and what it needs and to apply ourselves to those needs to the fullest.

Jesus said it another way, "You shall love the Lord your God with all your heart, soul, strength, and mind. And you shall love your neighbor as yourself" (Luke 10:27). When a person does that, he will succeed, for God will use his life to do great things.

11

The Preschool Child

What He Is Like

WHAT IS a preschool child like? He is sugar and spice. Sometimes the sugar rises to the top, sometimes the spice. When you're frustrated at the end of the day, the preschool child is noise with a runny nose and a knot in his shoestring. But later, when you tuck him in bed and his soft eyes meet yours, you forget all the problems. You're a total captive when he says softly, "I love you."

The preschool child hasn't yet learned to fight his way through a classroom of "friends." He hasn't yet been toughened by the day-by-day struggles of school and playground. He's still soft and sweet. At times he's a jar of twinkles from the farthest star. Or a sunbeam to cheer the dullest room.

He's softness, like the tattered blanket he sometimes carries around. He's cuteness, until he knows it. And he's as cuddly as the one-eyed panda bear at the foot of his bed.

Pack a hundred questions into a three-foot high bundle of noise, add a spoonful of mischief and a gallon of goodness, season it with witty sayings and exhibit it to the whole world as "ours" and you have a preschool child, ready to challenge you to new heights of leadership and love.

CHARACTERISTICS OF A PRESCHOOL CHILD

He has begun to see that he is a person, someone who can do things by himself. He can learn to tie his own shoes and put on his own clothes.

He has begun to see the difference between good and bad. He knows when he's done something bad and feels sorry about it. He's glad when he's done something good.

He has learned what punishment means, to be separated from the love and approval of his parents. He has also learned what forgiveness means, to be brought back into that love and approval.

He has learned to explore new sights and sounds, to broaden his world beyond his home and parents.

12

He has learned to play with others his own age. He takes part in a group now and contributes something to the group.

He has learned that he can please his parents by doing what is right and displease them by doing what is wrong.

He takes part in family life. He is beginning to add to the family conversation.

He has learned to depend on certain people and not on others. This helps him learn to depend on God also.

He has begun to learn many things about the world around him, and has many questions to help him understand them.

He has begun to ask questions about the strange questions of life, of birth and death, of sickness and health.

He has begun to use words well. He talks with others about his feelings and thoughts.

He has begun to lose his baby fat but he is still a little child in many ways. He still does not have enough coordination to draw or color the way he wants. This often makes him unhappy, for he knows what he wants to do, but has not developed the skill to do it.

Sometimes he still throws temper tantrums because he can't do something he wants to do. The wise parent or teacher will get his attention on to a new subject. The child will quickly forget his problem and enter the new subject with renewed interest.

He likes to do things by himself. When he succeeds, he likes to be praised. He likes to hear good comments about the things he has learned.

He is learning to take turns and to share with others. It is not an easy thing to learn, but he wants others to share with him.

He still lives in a make-believe world. Sometimes parents think a preschool child is lying when he is only talking about his make-believe world. Sometimes there is no difference between fact and fancy.

He has a short attention span. He cannot learn many things at one time. Nor does he remember them long, either.

What a Preschool Child
Can Learn

About God

God loves him
God takes care of him
God loves his mother and father
God takes care of his family
God sends the sunshine and rain
God helps food to grow
God does good things for people
God is all about him
God wants him to talk with Him
God made the world and all that is in it

About Jesus

Jesus loves him
Jesus once lived on earth, but is now in Heaven
Jesus is God's Son
Jesus is the Savior
Jesus is a Friend
Jesus said many good things which are in the Bible

About the Bible

The Bible is a friendly Book
The Bible tells us about God
The Bible is God's Word
The Bible tells about God's people
The Bible shows what God wants people to do
The Bible is a good Book to listen to

About Home and Parents

God gave parents to take care of him
God gave parents to show him what is right
God gave parents to teach him God's Word
God gave parents to pray for him and lead him
He should obey his parents
He should love his parents and try to please them

About Church and Sunday School

Church is a place to learn about God
Church is a place to sing about God
Church is a place to be with God's people
Church is a happy place
Church is a place to bring friends
Church is a place to learn about the Bible

About Others

God made all people, young and old
God loves all people, even those who do not love Him
God wants all people to love Him
God wants people to help others love Him
God wants him to be kind to others and share
God wants him to share his money at God's house
God wants him to pray for others
God wants him to love all other people
Others may sometimes be unkind to him
Others may not listen to him tell about Jesus
Others may not share as he does

The Child of Six and Seven

What He Is Like

WHAT is a child of six and seven like? He's a bridge, reaching across a wide gulf between "little child" and "big child." He's a doorway, standing between "home" and "the world." He's curiosity, with a mind like a sponge and hands like an octopus. Both are reaching out faster than he can take in.

A child of six and seven is imagination. In his mind a five-minute scribble with a ten-cent box of crayons is a masterpiece, filled with all kinds of specific details which only he can describe. But he is learning to draw and some of his masterpieces become quite good, for now you begin to actually see what he is trying to draw.

A child of six and seven is a confusing knot with two ends to the string. One end is tied to home and parents, the other end to the world around him. He wants to pull in each direction. A tug in one direction, and he wants to increase his independence, to step out more on his own. But a tug in the other direction, and he wants to feel the security of home and parents. A tug in both directions, and he becomes a tight little knot of confusion, waiting for life to help him get untied.

Six and seven is a launching pad from which a child skyrockets into the increasing complexities of the school years. Things move fast during these years, so the parents must move at jet speed with him.

HIS CHARACTERISTICS

He is learning to read now, which moves him from the world of "read-to-me" into the world of "I can do it." This makes him less dependent on mother or father and more dependent on self.

He loves to cut and paste, as well as color with crayons. His new skills help him create and express his thoughts in art. His expression is more specific now, changing from the scribbles of a preschool child to a picture which others can recognize. He's proud of his activity work and is glad when others compliment him on it.

16

He is restless and full of wiggles. Because he's growing so fast now, he wants to keep on the move. But his movement makes him tire easily and sometimes "get crabby" easily.

He is moving quickly into a big world. As a preschool child, his world was mostly home and family, perhaps a few neighborhood friends. But now he's part of a big, big world of school and community. It's natural that a little child in a big world will be afraid of a few things. The child of six and seven has more than his share of fears. Now, more than you may realize, or more than he may realize, he needs the security of love and attention. He needs to feel that mother and dad are with him, loving and helping him along the difficult road to independence.

He is learning more than ever to play with others his own age. But he finds it hard at times to share. As a preschool child, he did not have as many friends to share things with. Now it's a struggle to learn this important facet of life. The parent can help him realize that sharing pleases the parent and God.

He is learning about time and space. At times he may still feel that the parent grew up in "the olden days." But he is not quite sure how far back that goes. Don't be surprised if he places your childhood in early American history. It's hard for him to understand how far it is across the country and how long it takes to get there. He doesn't associate the road map with the hours of riding in the car, which may test his patience—and his parents'.

He is learning about death and Heaven and Hell. He can learn that Heaven is God's home and Hell is a place where bad people are punished. He can learn that Jesus can help us to go to Heaven and stay away from Hell. He can learn that bad things are sin and can keep us from living with God, that Jesus died to take away our sin, and that we can ask Him to do this. Many children this age have been saved and have grown in their spiritual lives.

He is learning to pray more specifically. That's because he is aware of more specific things for which he can pray. Encourage him to think of specific things for which he should thank God and specific people for whom he should pray. Help him think of specific prayer needs in his own life.

What the Child of Six and Seven Can Learn

About God

God loves him and his family and his friends
God loves all the people of the world
God wants people to love Him, too
God wants people to give their lives to Him
God provides food for men by letting plants grow
God takes care of the world He made
God is good, but He is also against evil
God wants us to pray and read our Bibles

About Jesus

Jesus is the Son of God
Jesus came to earth to die for sin
Jesus wants to help people go to God
Jesus wants to take sin from our lives
Jesus never did anything wrong
Jesus rose from the dead and lives in Heaven
Jesus loves us and wants to be our Friend

About the Bible

The Bible is God's Book, for it tells about Him
The Bible tells us what God wants
The Bible tells how God worked with others
The Bible tells much about us
The Bible is a good Book to learn, for it helps us
The Bible should be memorized

About Home and Parents

Parents are God's leaders for us on earth
Parents want to help us, so we should obey them
Parents love us, so we should love them, too
Parents provide food and clothing and home for us
God is an important guest in our home at all times

About Church and Sunday School

Church is God's house
Church is a place where God's people go
Church is a happy place
Church is a place for songs and prayer and Bible study
Church needs our help to keep it clean and quiet
Church is not just a building, but also the people

About Others

Others may want the same thing he does; he must share
Others may not want to do the same thing he does; he must
    learn to give in half way
Others may need something very much; he must learn to
    give
Others may be in trouble; he must learn to pray
Others may be unkind; he must learn to forgive
Others may not know Jesus; he must learn to tell them
    about Him

The Child of Eight and Nine

What He Is Like

WHAT is a child of eight and nine like? He's a "little adult" in his own eyes, but a "big girl or boy" in adult eyes. He's a flower unfolding into full bloom, beyond the "bud" stage of early childhood.

The child of eight and nine is a reader. He's far past the stage of "look" and "see" associated with the beginning reader. His reading takes him into a wide world of adventure and he loves it. He can be a pirate or a cowboy or a nurse without leaving the security of his own room. He can dream or imagine high adventure without stepping out on his own.

Eight and nine is an active child, a bundle of energy ready to explode into games or play. He's less interested in scissors, paste, and crayons now and more interested in hammering, sawing, sewing, knitting, drawing, and making things with his hands. He will keep on doing these things, too, until he does them well, for he's becoming more proud of his work. The wiggler has become a doer.

The knot in the string between home and the world is beginning to unwind away from home. The wide, wide world is beginning to pull, making him more independent each day, more ready for that later experience of "going out on his own."

HIS CHARACTERISTICS

He is asking many questions now, not just the who and what, but the why and how. He wants to know how things work and why some things happen. He looks to the parent for many of his answers. At this age he may especially be hurt if parents won't answer his questions.

He is curious about the wide world about him. He wants to handle some of the tools that Dad handles, or do some of the cooking that Mom does. Don't expect too much in his skills. He's just starting. But he is developing interests and that can last a lifetime. He needs help from Mother and Dad in developing the interests and skills which he will master later.

20

He is beginning to see why some things happen. He understands somewhat if told why he is being punished for something. He still won't like it, but he will see the parents' point of view a little more than before.

He can tell time now, but it still doesn't mean much to him. "Long ago" is indefinite. He still may think that the parents' childhood was in "olden" times or the early days of the nation.

He is aware of children of other countries and cultures. The world of people and their problems is opening up to him. He likes to know how boys and girls of other lands and cultures live. Early interests in missions and Bible-time people can be developed at this age.

He is more skillful now in the use of his body. He's able to throw a ball or jump with a rope. Games are fun now because he can do the skills they require. He likes to run and play with his friends. But he wants to do more than his body will let him. He wants to run faster and play longer and perform with more skill than he's ready to do.

He enjoys jokes now and likes to tell jokes. Sometimes he keeps on telling the same joke again and again. Humor is at its height when someone looks foolish because of something that happened.

He is hurt when others criticize him. He can't "back off" and look at himself objectively yet. He wants to be accepted, especially by his parents, while he struggles desperately to begin his move toward independence.

He has learned to worry. While six and seven feared the dark and the unknown around him, eight and nine worries about himself—how he is doing at school, problems at home, troubles with his friends, and his own personal problems.

He likes to be treated as a little adult in many ways. He doesn't want to have adults talk down to him or call him a little boy or girl. He really isn't a little boy or girl either, for he's at least half of the way toward being an adult.

He is coming to the age when he can make a definite decision to accept Christ into his life. He can begin to understand the plan of salvation and to see how important it is for him.

What the Child of Eight and Nine Can Learn

About God

God is all powerful, all wise and everywhere
God is present with him at all times
God wants to help him as he grows
God loves him and wants him to love God
God made the universe and all in it
God wants him to pray each day
God loves people all over the world

About Jesus

Jesus is the Son of God, the Savior
Jesus died on the cross for sin
Jesus can give salvation to those who ask
Jesus can forgive sin
Jesus wants him to be a disciple and follow Him

About the Bible

The Bible is an exciting Book to read
The Bible is a true Book, it is not fiction
The Bible is God's Word
The Bible should be read each day
The Bible has many important verses to be memorized
The Bible is God's truth
The Bible tells what God wants us to know

About the Home and Parents

Parents have rules for him to follow, but they also have
   God's rules to follow
Parents are to the child what God is to the parents
Parents want him to be a part of the family group
Home is a secure place where he can find his strength
Home is a happy place
Home is a place where he can talk over his problems with
   his parents
Home is a place where he can learn to follow rules

About Church and Sunday School

Church is like a school, except that he learns about God
   and the Bible
Church is a place where he can worship God
Church is a place to sing about God
Church is a place for families
Church is a happy place where he wants to go
Church needs his help to be all that it should

About Others

Others include a wider world, far beyond the community
Others include foreign boys and girls across the sea
Others need help, which he can give
Others need the Gospel, which he can share
Others need his prayers
Others need his money, which he can give

The Child of Ten and Eleven

What He Is Like

WHAT is a child of ten and eleven like? He's a jet pilot taking his plane through a crisis in the skies, a cowboy chasing robbers over the mountains, or a detective about to settle the most baffling case of all. He's imagination in living color, complete with sound effects and the energy to support it all. He's dirt, with a boy inside or lace and borrowed perfume with a girl in it. He's often called a junior.

A junior is frustration, if you're a parent. He's delight, if you're a grandparent or uncle or aunt. A junior boy brings giggles from a junior girl, but a junior girl brings grunts of disapproval from a junior boy.

A junior of ten and eleven is trying hard to be a teen-ager, while the teen-ager is trying hard for him not to be. To his younger brother or sister, he's a hero, but to his older brother or sister, he's a pest and a "kid."

A child of ten and eleven is a bundle of energy, about to burst into the explosive teen years. But he's God's opportunity for a Christian leader of tomorrow, so let's do all we can to put him in that important job.

HIS CHARACTERISTICS

His mind is a sponge, absorbing all he can learn. He sees many things, investigates, explores, and experiments with them. He wants to know. He wants you to help him know.

His sense of adventure is at a high point. He wants to explore new trails and find new experiences. What he can't do, because he is limited, he will imagine. Adventure stories capture his imagination. He enjoys the adventure of the Bible and likes to put himself in the place of great men.

He collects heroes, people he wants to "be like" when he gets older. His heroes could be good or bad, but they are people of action. He needs to become acquainted with the heroes of the Bible and learn to imitate their qualities of heroism.

He needs a challenge, for he wants to reach out and up. He's not willing

24

to settle for the ordinary. He's completely ready for the challenge to accept Jesus Christ and follow in His steps. This is the prime age to reach a child for Christ. Don't miss it and let these precious years go by.

The child of ten and eleven is competitive. He likes to play on a team. He loves to win and hates to lose, but he learns that a good player must sometimes be a good loser.

He is brave and daring and will try foolish stunts. He needs caution about foolishness, but not nagging.

He likes clubs and gangs and groups where he can organize and pursue some interesting goal. These are excellent years for Christian clubs and scouting.

He loves the great out of doors. He's thrilled to sit around a campfire on a summer night and watch the stars or listen to the wind in the trees. The Christian camp for boys has been one of the best settings for a decision to become a follower of Christ.

He loves to compete with others his own age. Bible memory can be fun when he's on a team, competing with others on another team.

He is loyal to friends and family. Loyalty to God is learned at this age, as well as loyalty to church and other believers.

He has learned the meaning of wrong and punishment. He knows what it means to be separated from one we love, one of the worst punishments of all. In this thought, he learns the tragic truth about Hell, eternal separation from the presence of God and His Son, Jesus Christ. This is the worst punishment we could ever have.

He reads his Bible well now. This is the age where each child should be given a very attractive copy of the Bible for his own. He should be encouraged to read it daily and seek to understand what it means to him and how he can put its truths to work.

He wants to think things through for himself. He should be encouraged to think about some of the great truths of the Bible and to think of ways he can put them to work in his life.

He can feel close to God as a person. He should be encouraged to pray for specific people and purposes. He needs help in knowing what to pray for and who to pray for.

What the Child of Ten and Eleven Can Learn

About God

God is a spirit, Who is everywhere, but Whose home is in Heaven.

God is all-powerful, but He permits evil things to happen.

God is all-wise, but He permits men to choose between Him and sin, even though He knows what is best.

God is one, but He has shown Himself in three ways, Father, Son (Jesus Christ), and Holy Spirit.

About Jesus

Jesus took on Himself the body of a man so He could do what God had planned

Jesus fulfilled part of God's great plan for the child, to bring him to God; the child must fulfil the other, to accept what Jesus did on the cross

Jesus shows the child of ten and eleven how to live for God, for His perfect life is a pattern for all

Jesus took the punishment for the sins of all men on Himself at Calvary

Jesus became alive again and lives in Heaven

About the Bible

The Bible has the answers to all his everyday problems

The Bible can help him live a happy life

The Bible tells the history of God's work among men

The Bible is God's Word, the authority for life

The Bible is set in the culture of another kind of people. He needs to understand that culture to understand the Bible

The Bible is a Book to honor and to memorize. It is God's truth to put into everyday practice

The Bible is God's truth for all men. He needs to share it with others

About Home and Parents

The home and parents are part of God's plan for him

The home and parents function as part of God's plan, but he should do his part, too

He should show loyalty to his home and parents

He should show honor to his home and parents

He should accept correction from his parents, for this will help him become a strong leader

He should begin to see what makes a Christian home, looking toward the day when he will start one

About Church and Sunday School

The church is a fellowship of believers in Christ

The church brings him in contact with Christian leaders

The church trains him in worship, study, prayer, witness, service and fellowship

The church is a place of opportunity to serve God

The church is a place where he can learn to practice Christian giving and outreach

About Others

Others need his respect for their thoughts, their possessions, their rights

Others need his understanding

Others need his help

He must show others honestly, loyalty, and fair play

Others need his forgiveness

Others need his prayers

Others fit into God's plans, just as he does

The Child of Twelve and Thirteen

What He Is Like

WHAT is a child of twelve and thirteen? He's a bottomless pit (boy) wired to 100 Amp. vocal cords. She's a sigh and a swoon (girl) with stars in her eyes.

Twelve is the exit ramp from childhood onto the teen-age expressway. Things move pretty fast from thirteen to eighteen. Growth spurts up at a rapid pace. Tastes change. Attitudes change. Life itself is a gigantic upheaval.

Twelve and thirteen are known for awkwardness. Growth is up more than out. They're often loud and boisterous. Girls move faster in their development than boys, but by the end of year thirteen, boys are shooting up rapidly.

Rapid growth brings skin problems, worries over new size, new height, new weight, and a new self-consciousness. It also brings a new kind of life with the change from childhood to manhood or womanhood.

HIS CHARACTERISTICS

He is a clown at times, making cracks about his friends, telling jokes, and teasing. He likes to see others make mistakes, for that is funny.

Sometimes he likes to sass and talk back. He may tell someone off or call names. If he gets angry enough, he throws things, tears things, or tries to get into a fight with brother or sister.

He sulks when things go wrong. If he doesn't get his way, he frowns, scowls, fusses, or gets angry. Sometimes he gets mean and unpleasant in his anger.

He is more organized in his work and arranges his time to fit it. He feels a sense of accomplishment when he works out problems by himself.

He likes to discuss and debate issues. He is more interested in issues on a national and international level, although not as much as he is later on.

He likes to read, but his tastes have changed from pure adventure to a

28

stronger emphais on the characters and their thoughts and insights. He is reaching the age where an adult book interests him occasionally. He is less interested in animal stories and more interested in detective, classics, sports, and mystery, as well as fiction, humor, and some poetry.

He likes to take part in group activity. This is the beginning age for young people's groups in church. Group projects and discussions are increasingly important for him as he grows older.

He tries to do right, but often realizes that he does wrong. Most of his wrongs are little things, such as not cleaning room, bad temper, laziness, poor table manners, not listening to orders, and fighting or getting angry at brothers and sisters.

He is less influenced by mother and may feel she is too critical now or doesn't give enough privileges. He gets along better with father, behaves better for him, but often doesn't feel as close to him.

He doesn't like to help much around home, but will do it reluctantly. He's willing to help, but not too happy about it.

He still argues and fights with those close to his own age in the family. Fighting is more often with words than fists.

He doesn't have as many special friends as he will later. He may like several and have them over for play. His friendships may change.

He has at last begun to show more interest in the opposite sex. Girls are more interested in boys than boys are in girls. In groups, boys may ignore girls or even act rough or rude to them.

He wants privacy, in his room, in his personal affairs, in his possessions, and in his secrets with friends.

Boys love sports and are wrapped up in them. Girls like bike rides or walks with friends, horses, skiing, and skating. Boys are interested also in hunting, fishing, and the outdoors.

What the Child of Twelve and Thirteen Can Learn

About God

God is always right, and just. He never changes. He keeps His promises.

God punishes and rewards people according to His justice. But God is always right in this.

God is to be honored and worshiped, even though He is sometimes difficult to understand.

God forgives when one has done wrong and turns to Him with true repentance.

About Jesus

God is revealed in Jesus Christ.

Jesus is the Savior, the Son of God, who can give a new life if one seeks it.

Following Jesus is not easy, but it can bring greater happiness than any other way.

Jesus died for his sins and wants to forgive those sins if he will ask for forgiveness.

About the Bible

The Bible is a revelation of God and His purposes and plans.

The Bible is a history of God's dealings with men.

The Bible is the authoritative Word of God.

The Bible is a collection of writings over many years from many authors, yet they were all inspired by God and fit together into one Book.

The Bible is a guide to daily living.

About Home and Family

Home and family are sacred institutions under God. He needs to learn respect for them.

Home and family are not complete without his presence and help. He must do his part.

Responsibilities at home are part of life. He must accept them and do them cheerfully.

Even though he is struggling to be free from adult guidance, he must appreciate it and thank God for it.

Brothers and sisters are given by God for a purpose. He needs to learn appreciation for them.

About Church and Sunday School

The local church is part of the larger church, made up of all believers.

The local church is part of a great history of the church which has brought him freedom to worship.

The local church is God's representative in the community. It is an organization composed of believers who want to reach out into the community with God's message.

The local church is a group of believers, meeting together for worship, prayer, Bible study, and mutual help.

About Others

Working together for Christ helps to strengthen each other.

Christian standards can be applied to a group, even if the group is not made up of Christians. The child can remember that he belongs to Christ and that he should conduct himself as a true believer.

The group can contribute some things which the home cannot.

Friendships are important if they are true friendships; but are poor if based on money, social status, or what the friend can do for him.

Others need him and his message about Jesus Christ.

The Child of Fourteen and Fifteen

What He Is Like

WHAT is a child of fourteen and fifteen like? He's making one last desperate effort to shed his childhood. He's beyond the spanking age and he knows it. But he hasn't reached the age of adult responsibility, and he knows that, too.

Fourteen and fifteen are difficult ages, for so much growth is taking place. By the time a girl is fifteen, she has grown about as much as she will grow. The boy of fifteen has reached about 90% or more of his growth.

Fourteen and fifteen are settling down into mental growth. They're trying to discover who they are, what they're doing here on earth, and where they're going, and so on. The physical turmoil of early teens has passed, only to bring on a new turmoil, that of the mind and life's purpose.

The awkwardness of the early teen body has given way now to the awkwardness of a growing personality. If your mid-teen seems silly, sarcastic, impatient, indifferent, self-conscious, and intolerant, it's probably because most of the boys and girls his age have the same problems.

HIS CHARACTERISTICS

He is noisy and rowdy at times. Boys show off. Girls gather to talk and
giggle. He's full of energy and lets it overflow in all that he does.

He is activity minded. He likes to plan far-reaching activities. Many of
them can be carried out and some will have to wait. It's not uncommon
to plan too much for his capacity, then find that he can't do it all.

Boys this age are absorbed in athletics. Girls are absorbed in watching
boys in athletics. Much attention is given to school athletic programs
—basketball, football, tennis, swimming, and others.

He is concerned with his personal appearance. Skin blemishes embarrass
him. Voice changes and other physical changes make him self-con-
conscious.

32

His humor changes to a more sarcastic, or dry humor. He likes to imitate, to ridicule, and to insult. Mimicry and irony are favorites, too.

He lets his anger come out in mean and catty words. He calls names, snaps back with mean remarks, and yells at the person who has made him angry.

He worries often about school, his grades, his homework, his popularity, and many things in general.

He talks noisily when he does talk. Sometimes he is moody and quiet. At other times he chatters noisily with others. Boys like to horse around with one another.

He has many questions to ask about "why" and "how." He's trying to think issues through more clearly and to come to his own convictions. He doesn't want to accept what adults say just because adults are saying it. He wants to make up his own mind.

He wants to know more about himself and what he is like. He is struggling to meet the high ideals he has set for himself.

He reads more in the adult line of books now. Girls like adult novels with romance in them. Boys quietly tolerate it, but still prefer sports, mystery, and adventure. He is beginning to read the newspapers, and takes an interest in current events.

He doesn't like advice too much. He would rather learn by trial and error, mostly error. Failure is an important teacher and helps him grow.

He likes to be treated as an adult. He wants people to talk to him as an adult and think of him as an adult.

He may seek responsibility, such as getting a job so he can earn money for special projects. Boys like special hobbies, such as photography, radios, carpentry, or models. Girls like sewing, cooking, letter writing, and telephoning.

He is forming habits and patterns of life which will affect his future career and marriage and Christian conduct.

What the Child of Fourteen and Fifteen Can Learn

About God

God is a real person, not just a vague idea, Someone who affects his daily life.

God is more than a philosophy. He is a loving Person who wants to be personally involved with his life.

The character of God is revealed in the Bible.

God knows what He is doing, even though the young person may want to question some of the things God does.

God wants him to repent of sin and turn to Him for forgiveness through Jesus Christ.

About Jesus

Jesus' mission to earth was to redeem lost men.

Jesus was born of a virgin mother, Mary. God was His Father.

Jesus' death paid the price for sin. But each person must apply that death benefit to his life.

Jesus was the Messiah for whom the Jews waited so long. As Messiah, He came for the special job God had planned for Him, to save all who would repent.

About the Bible

The Bible speaks to all the issues of life.

The Bible answers all the questions of life.

The Bible meets all the needs of life.

The Bible was set in another culture, but it has a timeless message for men today.

The Bible was inspired by God and is His Word.

About Home and Family

The home and family is the training ground of life. Many attitudes and habits of life are developed here.

The family is an institution ordained by God.

The family needs the cooperation of all members.

Marriage is a sacred relationship, established by God. Sex in marriage is not dirty, but part of God's plan.

Marriage is not to be entered into lightly. It is a serious relationship, one that can bring great honor to God.

About a third of all marriages end in divorce. The percentages of teen marriages are higher. Couples need Christ to help them succeed in marriage.

About Church and Sunday School

Church is a place of opportunity, where God can work with the needs of people.

Church is a focal point of Christian outreach.

Church needs each member to do its work. All members must work and pray together in harmony.

Church is a center for Bible study, prayer, and Christian witnessing.

About Others

Adults have problems, just as teen-agers do. They need understanding and prayers also.

Adults have contributed much to bring him to this point. He needs to show them honor and respect for their part in his growth.

Parents have been self-sacrificing in raising him. Now that he is becoming more independent, he needs to show them respect and honor for what they have done.

Others deserve his appreciation, cooperation, and help. They do not deserve discrimination, criticism, and unkind feelings.

Others need Christ. Some may never hear unless he tells them. He has a responsibility to others.

The Child of Sixteen and Seventeen

What He Is Like

WHAT is a child of sixteen and seventeen like? He's not really a child anymore, not in the sense that we think of children. Most young people this age are fully developed physically. They're mentally adult and show adult manners in much of their activities.

But there are times when "the child" shows through. Touches of immaturity come to the surface from time to time. The so-called generation gap points out to his parents and others that he has not fully accepted the adult world, and perhaps the adult world has not fully accepted him.

Young people of sixteen and seventeen sometimes marry and have children of their own. They drive cars and get jobs. They apply to colleges they hope to enter shortly, or explore some branch of the services they would like to join.

Parental guidance tapers off drastically at this age. The parent has less opportunity than ever to shape his child's thoughts or habits by the time the young person reaches this age.

Even though the young person of sixteen and seventeen is better equipped than at any time in previous history, he lacks two important qualities which would place him in the adult world—experience and judgment based on experience. He must depend on his adult leaders for these two, and for their prayers!

HIS CHARACTERISTICS

He is more easygoing than before. The tensions of growing up physically are over. Girls of sixteen and seventeen are fully matured physically. Boys are almost matured, except perhaps for further muscle development.

He is in better control of his temper than previously. Doesn't get angry as quickly as fourteen or fifteen does. He may brood when he becomes angry, or sulk alone in his room.

36

He understands and appreciates adult humor now. He likes the subtle touches of humor.

He is able to reason now. He can think something through quite logically. He sees how different relationships fit together. But he still lacks good judgment. He has not had enough experience to give him the basis for good judgment.

He is a doer rather than a reader. He reads more magazines and newspapers than books. When he does read books, novels, sports, mystery, humor, and classics are favorites.

He likes to make plans and carry them out. He enjoys making independent plans, based on independent thinking.

He thinks much about his career and his future. He wonders about his future husband or wife, what kind of a job he will get, where he should go to college, what he should take as a major subject, and what he should do with his life.

He plans more activities away from the family. His independence takes him more and more into his own circles of friends, school groups, young peoples' church groups, and others. This is part of his natural process of growing away from home and parents into his own life. It is natural, and parents must expect it, even though it may be painful for them to see their child "cut the cord" and leave them.

He is at the age where he begins to date. Some young people date earlier, but most begin their dating during these years.

He resists advice from adults because he is reaching for his own independence. If he listens to an adult, it is usually someone other than parents. This is one reason why a youth leader is so important in the church. He can become a Christian counselor to the late teen, helping him see the Christian point of view on his problems.

He is conscious of success and wants to succeed in whatever he does. He wants recognition for his success.

He gets along well with his family now, and has developed a better attitude toward Mother. At fourteen and fifteen, he felt Mother was restricting him too much, but now she is letting up some, perhaps because he does not require as much supervision. But the young person still does not help much at home, and sometimes seems lazy and disinterested.

What the Child of Sixteen and Seventeen Can Learn

About God

This is the age to finalize his commitment to God, seeking God's guidance for his choice of a mate and career.

About Christ

The sixteen and seventeen-year-old can learn the full meaning of discipleship, following Jesus Christ.

About the Bible

He is at a focal point where he should develop life-long habits of Bible reading and Bible study.

About Home and Parents

Although he is cutting the ties with home and family, he should be gaining an appreciation for all that home and family has done for him. He should be looking toward the establishment of his own Christian home and family.

About Church and Sunday School

He should have a more active involvement in the plans and programs of the church and Sunday School.

About Others

He should begin to develop habits of prayer for others, help for others, witnessing for others, and respect for others.

A Guide

---

to Life's Questions

Questions
About Drugs

PARENTS TODAY are frightened by the drug problem. They have every reason to be. Young people by the hundreds of thousands are looking for new thrills by "turning on" with drugs. This has become a nightmare to parents across the country.

If you're close enough to your child, he may ask you for answers to his questions about drugs. Would you have to tell him, "I don't know?" To him it may sound like "I don't care." He may not ask again. The next person he asks may be the wrong person! Of course you would not want that for your children.

You, as a concerned parent, must be concerned enough to get the facts. The following material will help to introduce you to the subject. It will also direct you to additional help. A few hours of study now may save you days of grief later.

What Are Drugs?

The broad use of the word includes many products on the shelf at the drug store. Vitamins, cough drops, and first aid cream are "drugs" in the broad sense. But we don't get frightened by them because they are not often used in the wrong way to harm people.

What Are Prescription Drugs?

Prescription drugs are those which require a doctor's prescription. Since they must be used in a more specific way, the doctor must "prescribe" what they are to be used for and how they are to be used. When used in the right way, prescription drugs can save lives, relieve pain, and reduce suffering.

What Is "the Drug Problem?"

The drug problem is usually thought to be the misuse or abuse of drugs. It is the use of drugs for the wrong purposes. The drug problem becomes more and more serious as it moves into a habit, then dependence, then addiction.

40

What Is a Drug Habit?

The drug habit means a psychological desire to use drugs again and again. The body does not yet demand drugs, but it would be hard to stop doing it because the mind wants a repeat performance. The drug habit is kept up because the person *wants* to do it.

What Is Drug Dependence?

Drug dependence is the next step down the drug ladder. It means that a person has come to depend on the drug to keep going. His dependence may be either mental or physical, but he does need to keep taking them to keep up his false sense of well-being. This person may keep on drugs because he *wants* to, or because he *has* to.

What Is Drug Addiction?

Drug addiction means the physical dependence on a drug. The body has adjusted itself to the use of this drug in such a way that it requires its continued use.

To stop using the drug can bring on serious physical symptoms, such as convulsions or vomiting. But the longer a person is addicted to a drug, the more he must use to produce the same effect. The addict rides a nightmarish merry-go-round which goes faster and faster, trapping him deeper and deeper into its machinery.

Which Drugs Are Harmful?

Any drug can be harmful if used wrongly or if too much is used. Many adults have committed suicide by taking too many "harmless" sleeping pills.

Many "harmless" drugs are harmful when taken together with other drugs, or when taken by people who are too sensitive to them. Treat all drugs with respect and use them for the purpose for which they were intended, and in the amount in which they were intended!

Which People Are Involved in the Drug Problem?

There are communities of young people who live together and practice bad habits, including the drug problem. But this problem has also invaded almost every community of the country, causing young people living at home to use drugs.

But many adults are part of the drug problem also. It is not limited to the young alone.

Why Do People Misuse Drugs?

The drug problem involves people who are unhappy, bored, or in some way dissatisfied with life. Some are dissatisfied with their own performance in life—bad grades, lack of success, lack of any clear-cut purpose, or unhappiness in their friendships. Others are dissatisfied with their family, or the society in which they live. There's a void in those people's lives. Drugs offer them a false hope and they try for it. The sad part of this story is that nobody has told them about the deep and lasting happiness which they could have in Jesus Christ. Nobody has brought the Good News to them!

KINDS OF HARMFUL DRUGS

What Are the Different Kinds of Drugs Which Are Misused?

The drug problem involves many kinds of drugs. Generally these are classified as narcotics, barbiturates (depressants), amphetamines (stimulants), and hallucinogens.

NARCOTICS

What Is a Narcotic?

A narcotic is some form of opium, or a synthetic drug which produces the same effect. Opium is produced from the poppy plant. It is used legally in pain-killing medicines.

There are other drugs produced from opium, also used legally for pain-killing. These are codeine, morphine, paregoric, and heroine.

Cocaine, made from coca leaves, and marijuana are classified as narcotics by law, although chemically they are not.

Narcotics are extremely dangerous when misused and can result in death. A person who becomes "hooked" on narcotics is an addict. He must have larger and larger doses to get the same effects.

What Is So Dangerous About Narcotics?

When the body gets hooked on narcotics, it demands their use in larger and larger quantities. Since these are usually obtained illegally, addiction becomes very expensive. People are driven to commit crimes in order to support their addiction. Many girls are forced to become

42

prostitutes to earn enough money to pay for narcotics. Boys are forced to steal, or to commit other crimes, for an addict may require as much as $100 a day for his drugs.

Since the addict spends almost all his time supporting his addiction, he finds it difficult, if not impossible, to hold a job or finish his education. Addiction also makes him sick frequently, causing him to have time off from work or school.

The narcotics addict has a change in personality. He is no longer the same person. This means that his friends change also.

Narcotics addiction shortens life by at least fifteen to twenty years. Sometimes an addict dies from an overdose.

What Other Trouble Can the Addict Have?

There is a law (the Harrison Act of 1914) which sets stiff penalties for the illegal possession or illegal sale of narcotics.

Illegal possession of narcotics can bring two to ten years in prison for a first time, five to twenty years for a second time, and ten to twenty years in prison for more than two times.

Illegal sale of narcotics can bring a prison sentence of from five to twenty years for a first time, ten to forty years for more than one time. The illegal sale of heroine to a youngster under eighteen can bring life imprisonment or death.

What Can a Youngster Lose by Taking Narcotics?

The tragic answer is that he can lose everything. Here are a few specific things he can lose:

1. He can lose his own individual personality, for he is likely to have a personality change.
2. He can lose all his friends.
3. He can lose his freedom, for addiction can make him a slave.
4. He can lose his job, because he is too preoccupied in getting drugs and is often sick from drugs.
5. He can lose his education, because he loses his interest in studying.
6. He can lose his future, for without an education or a good job, there isn't much to look forward to.
7. He can lose his family, for often he may turn against his family because they do not share his new ideas.

8. He can lose his morals, for he may have to steal or commit other crimes to support his drug use.
9. He can lose his life, for drugs have caused many deaths across the country in the past few years.

There is so little to gain, so much to lose. Help your children see the high price of drug abuse.

BARBITURATES

What Are Barbiturates?

Barbiturates are part of a large group of drugs called sedatives. Sedatives are used by doctors to help calm the central nervous system. They have been helpful to people with nervous disorders. But barbiturates have been misused by many as part of the drug problem.

Doctors prescribe barbiturates for people who have high blood pressure, insomnia, or epilepsy. They are also used to help relax the human body to prepare it for surgery. Used properly under a doctor's care, barbiturates can be very helpful.

What Do Barbiturates Do?

They slow down the heart, breathing, and blood pressure. They reduce the actions of nerves, heart muscle, and skeletal muscle.

Then Why Are Barbiturates Dangerous?

When doses of barbiturates are increased beyond the safe level, they cause harmful effects. The user appears to be drunk. He loses part of his ability to think and work. He loses control of his emotions and may do things he would normally not do. He may try to hurt someone he would normally not want to hurt. Barbiturates also change the way things seem, and thus have caused many serious automobile accidents. Barbiturates are physically addicting. If an addict stops using them, he may have nausea, cramps, convulsions, or delirium. Overdoses of barbiturates can cause death.

AMPHETAMINES

What Are Amphetamines?

Barbiturates slow down the nervous system. Amphetamines speed it up. Some people call these drugs "uppers" and "downers" because of their effect on the human body. Other people call them "up and down drugs."

Amphetamines are drugs which stimulate the nervous system. They increase the heart rate, raise the blood pressure, and depress the appetite. They are prescribed in mild doses by doctors to help in weight reduction programs or to combat fatigue and sleepiness during an emergency. They are also prescribed in small quantities to control depression.

How Are Amphetamines Misused?

Amphetamines become part of the drug problem when they are misused. Athletes sometimes use them before a sporting event to speed up bodily functions, even though sporting associations have made rules against their use. Truck drivers often take them to keep awake on long trips. Housewives and businessmen and other adults in various walks of life take them to "give them a lift." These uses border on abuses and can be considered part of the drug problem also.

Young people have created the most serious abuse of amphetamines. Many have turned to amphetamines to "turn on." This is done by overdoses or by injecting liquid amphetamines into a vein. This is called "speeding," and can be very dangerous.

What Are the Dangers of Amphetamine Abuse?

Although amphetamines do not normally cause physical addiction, they may cause psychological dependence, getting used to the drugs in such a way that one "can't do without" their effects. Amphetamines in large doses can stretch the body beyond safe limits. They may cause a temporary mental derangement in which the user hears or sees things that are not really happening. They also cause a breakdown of the emotions, the intellect, and social relationships. Withdrawing from overdoses may cause a person to become so depressed that he wants to commit suicide. "Speed" in high doses can cause death.

HALLUCINOGENS

What Are Hallucinogens?

A hallucinogen is a drug which causes hallucinations, hearing or seeing things which do not really exist. Two of the most common are LSD and Peyote. Others include mescaline, psilocybin, DMT and STP.

What Is LSD?

LSD is a research drug, developed for the study of mental illness. Some think it will be used later to help alcoholics and those with various kinds of mental disorders. It is used legally only for research purposes at this time. LSD is chemically lysergic acid diethylamide. It is so powerful that one ounce provides three hundred thousand doses! A dose is one speck, usually taken on a cracker, cookie, or sugar cube.

What Does LSD Do?

LSD causes the heart to beat faster, the blood pressure to rise, body temperature to rise, and hands and feet to shake. The palms become sweaty and cold, the face grows pale and flushed, and nausea usually sets in.

Colors grow stronger and very brilliant. Colorful patterns come to the user. The senses become confused so that music can be seen as colors or colors may be tasted. Two opposite emotions, such as happiness and sadness, may be felt at the same time. The user loses a sense of time and may sense strange mystical feelings.

Why Is LSD Dangerous?

LSD is a very dangerous drug. It can bring great fear to a person when he cannot "shut off" the action when he wants to. He may be terrified, thinking he is losing his mind. For two or three days after using LSD, the person may think that others are trying to harm or control him and may become very suspicious of those about him.

LSD has a danger of recurring action. Days, weeks, or months after a "trip" the things that the user imagined may come back suddenly. Often he may become terrified, thinking he is going insane.

An LSD trip, the experience the user has when he takes LSD, may cause the person to think that he can do anything. He may step in front of a speeding car or jump from a high window, thinking that he will not get hurt.

Researchers have not proven it yet, but there is strong evidence that LSD may harm an unborn child. Many deformed children have been born to young mothers who have used LSD. A more frightening result may also be the altering of the hereditary chain, so that unborn generations may be different, perhaps harmed in unknown ways, by the effects of LSD used in one person today.

46

LSD can have such serious effects on the growing mind that it can leave permanent mental illness in the user. Severe worry, panic and depression, as well as mental derangement can result. These conditions sometimes lead to suicide.

What Is Peyote?

Peyote is a drug which comes from a cactus plant by that name. The cactus plant is cut into slices and allowed to dry. These dried slices are called "buttons." The plant contains mescaline, which gives the user hallucinations, similar to those of LSD. Peyote buttons are often chopped and made into a tea or used with wine to kill their unpleasant taste.

What Is Mescaline?

Mescaline is a substance derived from a cactus plant. It is similar to LSD and peyote in its effects.

MARIJUANA

What Is Marijuana?

Marijuana, often called "pot," is a drug obtained from the Indian hemp plant. This plant grows in many countries of the world, including the United States. The leaves and flowers of the hemp plant are dried, then broken into small pieces and smoked in the same way as tobacco, either in pipes or in cigarettes. As it enters the bloodstream, the drug affects thinking and mood. It produces a faster heart beat, a lower body temperature, and sugar levels in the blood. The user may be more depressed or more excited. Time and distance may be distorted as well as judgment. The overall effect is a form of intoxication.

Do People Become Addicted to Marijuana?

Marijuana users do not become addicted physically. But they may become dependent psychologically. Because marijuana is not addictive, does not require larger doses for the same effect, and does not leave dangerous withdrawal symptoms, many people think it is safe. But they are not thinking of the other dangerous possibilities of its use.

What Are the Dangers of Marijuana?

Marijuana users enjoy comparing the drug they use with alcohol and tobacco. They like to speak of the hypocrisy of those who smoke and drink, but criticize marijuana. Perhaps they are right in their criticism, for all three of these substances can be very dangerous. It is true that an alcoholic or a habitual smoker may be hurting himself more than the marijuana user.

But it is also true that the marijuana user may be seriously hurting himself! That is hypocrisy, too, when a person hides behind the faults of others.

One serious danger of marijuana is the unknown. There is simply not enough known about it today to say that it is safe. A number of years ago, tobacco was in the same place. Today it is condemned as a great danger to health, especially in contributing to cancer. Marijuana may be a serious threat to health in some way which is not yet known.

Another serious danger of marijuana is the impure materials mixed with it. Since it is not under the control of food and drug authorities, dangerous substances can be mixed with it, intentionally or unintentionally.

If a marijuana peddler is also a hard-drug peddler, he may mix enough narcotics with the marijuana to get the marijuana user "hooked" on hard drugs. Then it is too late. It is a fact that about 80% of those on heroin started with marijuana.

Unlike other drugs, marijuana has no known medical use. It is used exclusively "for kicks."

What Can a Person Lose by Taking Marijuana?

1. He can lose his own mental freedom, for he may find that he becomes psychologically dependent on it.
2. He can lose all that a narcotics user may lose, for there is always the possibility that he may advance into narcotics.
3. He may lose his social freedom, for the law provides two to forty years in prison for possessing marijuana, ten to forty years in prison for selling it.
4. If convicted of possessing marijuana, a young person can also lose the right to vote, to own a gun, to run for public office, to work for city, state, or federal government, to enter West Point, Annapolis, or the Air Force Academy. He cannot become a doctor, dentist, attorney, detective, public official, pharmacist, certified public accountant, or any one of many responsible careers. He may also lose family and friends. These are high prices to pay for a few thrills!

WHERE TO GET ADDITIONAL INFORMATION

Here are some sources for additional information if you wish to study more about the drug problem.

National Clearinghouse for Drug Abuse Information
5454 Wisconsin Avenue
Chevy Chase, Maryland 20015

Bureau of Narcotics & Dangerous Drugs
U.S. Department of Justice
Washington, D.C. 20537

Superintendent of Documents
U.S. Government Printing Office
Washington, D.C. 20402

National Education Association
Publication-Sales Department
1201 Sixteenth St., N.W.
Washington, D.C. 20036

American Medical Association
535 North Dearborn Street
Chicago, Illinois 60610

American Pharmaceutical Association
2215 Constitution Ave., N.W.
Washington, D.C. 20037

Blue Cross and Blue Shield Plans
222 N. Dearborn Street
Chicago, Illinois 60601

Pharmaceutical Manufacturers Assoc.
1155 Fifteenth Street, N.W.
Washington, D.C. 20013

World Health Organization
Twenty-third St. and Virginia Ave., N.W.
Washington, D.C. 20032

Many publications may be purchased from these and other organizations at a small cost. Some are free. Ask for a list before ordering.

WHAT'S THE ANSWER TO THE DRUG PROBLEM?

A person usually turns to drugs to fill some void or emptiness in his life. He may lack a happy home life or a satisfying school relationship. He may have a lack of purpose in life. This is one of the most serious deficiencies of all.

It's possible for someone to turn to drugs to please a friend or to satisfy his curiosity. He might also turn to drugs as a rebellion against home or society. But if a person is truly happy in his personal life and his home life, the chances of his turning to drugs are extremely low.

Parent, this is your responsibility and challenge. Life's greatest purpose comes with a dedication of yourself to Jesus Christ. If you are an earnest Christian, you will be happy. If you are a happy Christian, fulfilling an important purpose for Him, this will show in your home and to your children. Your child will want to become a follower of Christ, too. There is no desire for drugs in a happy Christian home. Try this, and you will agree that this is the best answer to the drug problem!

DICTIONARY OF DRUG TERMS

ACID, LSD
ACIDHEAD, someone who uses LSD
BARBS, barbiturates
BUSTED, arrested
COLD TURKEY, getting off drugs suddenly
COP OUT, to stop taking drugs or to confess
FIX, narcotics injection
GRASS, marijuana
HIGH, under drug influence
HOOKED, addicted
JUNKIE, narcotics addict
MAINLINE, injecting drugs into a vein
POT, marijuana
PUSHER, a drug peddler
REEFER, marijuana cigarette
SPEED, methamphetamine
SPEED FREAK, someone who injects amphetamines in large doses
TURNED ON, under drug influence
UPPERS, stimulants such as amphetamines
WEED, marijuana

50

Questions About Alcohol

WHY ALL THE FUSS about drinking? Isn't everyone doing it? These are questions frequently asked. The truth is that many people are doing it, but not everyone, of course. And drinking is such a serious problem that it demands a fuss.

The drinking of alcohol is one of the most serious problems facing our nation. It may be as serious as the drug problem. Some think it is even more serious because there are few legal restrictions placed upon it and because the adult world not only accepts it, but glamorizes it. Just how serious is the alcohol problem? These questions and answers may help you understand more about it.

What Is Alcohol?

Alcohol, as it appears in "drinks," is a depressant narcotic drug. It is "Ethyl Alcohol," shown chemically as C_2H_5OH or C_2H_6O. It is not a food. It is not a stimulant. It is not a tonic. It has no proteins, no vitamins, and no food value. It has only calories.

What's Wrong With Drinking Alcohol?

Like drugs, alcohol can create some serious problems for you and those about you. Here are some of them:

1. IT DULLS THE BRAIN

Alcohol is a depressant which slows down many important functions of the brain. It affects our control of the body. Too much alcohol causes people to do things they would never do otherwise. It affects the speech, equilibrium, emotions, and even vision. It slows down or dulls the sense of caution and causes people to take foolish chances or do dangerous things.

2. IT CREATES SOME SERIOUS HEALTH PROBLEMS

Alcohol has no food value, but makes the body work just as hard to process it and eliminate it. Beriberi, pellagra, and cirrhosis of the

51

liver may come to people who depend too much on alcohol. Cirrhosis of the liver occurs six times as much in heavy drinkers as in others. The liver may be seriously damaged by the heavy drinking of alcohol.

3. IT CREATES A SERIOUS SAFETY HAZARD

In 1970, auto accidents in the United States killed 55,400 persons, more than all the United States' casualties in World War I. During that one year, 4,950,000 people in the United States were injured by automobile accidents. A recent survey by the State of Illinois found that 76% of the fatal accidents in the state resulted from persons with alcohol in their blood. This shows that hundreds of thousands of people are dying and millions are being injured because people drink and drive.

4. IT CREATES SERIOUS FAMILY PROBLEMS

Heavy drinkers often become difficult to live with. They may become abusive, or moody, or withdrawn. They may use large amounts of money needed for food or clothing. Drinking takes them away from home and family and fixes their interests in other places and activities. Alcohol causes a high percentage of divorces.

5. IT CREATES MUCH OF THE CRIME IN THE COUNTRY

Estimates show that 16% to 75% of all crime is caused by alcohol. One of every three arrests in the country is for drunkenness. It has been estimated that $100,000,000 is spent each year just to arrest and handle drunks. These arrests clog the courts and keep people with serious needs from getting justice quickly, they burden police departments and take the police away from other more important duties, and they place a serious blight on our whole legal system.

6. IT PLACES A BURDEN ON BUSINESS AND INDUSTRY

Officials estimate that business and industry lose $4,000,000,000 each year because of alcohol. People with alcohol problems either do not report for work or cause waste and lost production when they do show up.

7. IT CAUSES WIDESPREAD MENTAL HEALTH PROBLEMS

One state mental hospital reported that 50% of all persons admitted were there because of alcohol. "D.T.'s," or Delirium Tremens, often result from nerve damage due to too much heavy drinking. This mental problem causes hallucinations and shaking. Serious damage to the nervous system and the brain can come from too much alcohol, resulting in lifelong problems.

8. IT CAUSES SPIRITUAL PROBLEMS

Alcoholism destroys a person's relationship to God. The two simply do not mix. Jesus said, "No man can serve two masters: for either he will hate the one, and love the other; or else he will hold to the one, and despise the other" (*Matthew 6:24*). Alcoholism is a master. It takes control of a person and makes him a slave. No man can serve both alcohol and God.

9. IT BRINGS AN EARLIER DEATH

About half of the alcoholics, people with serious alcohol habits, die before they are fifty. If alcohol doesn't get a person killed in an auto accident, or sent to a mental institution, it may well cause death from a breakdown of health.

What Is an Alcoholic?

An alcoholic is a person who allows alcohol to become his master. He becomes dependent on alcohol and "must have it" to keep going.

Are There Many Alcoholics?

There are between six and seven million alcoholics in America. The average alcoholic has four others in the family, which means that from twenty-four to twenty-eight million Americans live in an alcoholic home. This does not include all the additional millions of brothers, sisters, mothers, fathers, aunts, uncles, and other near relatives who are "in the family" of an alcoholic.

Why Is It So Bad To Be An Alcoholic?

Consider again all the problems of drinking as given above. Then consider that an alcoholic is sold out to these things. He is a slave to them. He has permitted alcohol to control his life like a master.

Can An Alcoholic Be Cured?

No, an alcoholic is an alcoholic as long as he lives. Medically, there is no "cure" for it. An alcoholic may find ways to stay away from drink, but if he ever tries to become a social drinker again, he will likely become a heavy drinker.

Many people have found their only "cure" is a new life in Jesus Christ. This is a "cure" because it helps the alcoholic change masters. When he is sold out to Christ, he has a new strength to fight off the desire to drink. As long as he lets Christ help him in that fight, he can withstand the temptation to drink. If he tries to fight his problem in his own strength, he may go back to drink again. Some people have succeeded in staying away from drink through their own determination, but it is a difficult battle. How much easier it is when Christ dwells within to give added strength to resist. Prayer is one of the greatest helps in conquering the alcohol problem. So is Christian fellowship with those who understand and pray with the person who needs them.

Where Can I Get Extra Literature About Alcohol?

Alcoholics Anonymous World Services, Inc.
Box 459, Grand Central Station
New York, New York 10017

Blue Cross and Blue Shield
222 North Dearborn St.
Chicago, Illinois 60601

Rutgers Center of Alcohol Studies
New Brunswick, N.J. 08903

National Center for Prevention and Control of Alcoholism
National Institute of Mental Health
Chevy Chase, Maryland 20015

American Medical Association
535 North Dearborn St.
Chicago, Illinois 60610

Preferred Risk Mutual Insurance Company
West Des Moines, Iowa 50265
(Auto insurance company for non-drinkers)

Al-Anon Family Group Headquarters
Post Office Box 182
Madison Square Station
New York, New York 10010

Alcohol Education Foundation
515 North 6th Street
Springfield, Illinois 62702

Questions About Tobacco

ALONG WITH DRUGS and alcohol, tobacco is one of the most urgent health problems of our day. Smoking has created such a health problem that the government no longer permits the advertisements for cigarettes to be broadcast on television. Here are some facts which you and your children should know about tobacco.

Are Cigarettes Really Dangerous?

Tobacco contains tars which can produce cancer. When smoke is inhaled into the lungs the tissue cells change. In many cases, the lung cells change from normal, healthy ones to cancerous cells. Studies have shown clearly that there is a direct connection between lung cancer and cigarette smoking.

There is also evidence that cigarette smoking increases heart disease, chronic bronchitis, and another serious lung disease called emphysema. Thus, many health problems come from smoking.

Will Cigarettes Kill You?

The evidence which has been gathered by research shows that the smoker cannot expect to live as long as the non-smoker. For every one hundred non smokers who die, one hundred and seventy smokers die. Or, to put it another way, the death rate is seventy per cent higher for smokers.

Why Can't I Smoke Just a Little?

Because cigarettes are habit forming. Ask people who have tried to quit. With some it seems almost impossible.

Won't It Be All Right If I Smoke Filter Tips?

No method of treating tobacco or filtering smoke will eliminate the hazard of lung cancer, according to information from the U.S. Surgeon General's office. Filters may reduce the problem, but they do not eliminate it completely.

But What If People Call Me Chicken or Sissy For Not Smoking?

It takes a "man" or "woman" to say no to something wrong. Any chicken or sissy can give in. The real sissies and chickens are the people who do not have the courage to say no.

Why Shouldn't I Smoke?

Here are some of the reasons why smoking is not good for you. There are others which you may think of.

1. There is definitely a risk of shortening your life, not only from lung cancer, but from the other health problems as well, such as heart disease and emphysema.

2. Smoking becomes a habit, therefore it becomes the smoker's master. Smokers who want to quit later find it extremely difficult, almost impossible to do so.

3. Smoking causes many small discomforts, such as helping to kill the taste of food, aggravating the throat and mouth and causing coughing, shortening the breath, causing some people to be dizzy because of the nicotine, causing others to be irritable or nervous, and often impairing vision.

4. Smoking is expensive. A two-pack-a-day smoker will spend as much as $300 per year for his habit. If he smokes for fifty years, he will spend about $15,000 for cigarettes. Think of all the worthwhile things he could have done with that money! Think how much interest he could have earned with this money!

5. Smoking is unpleasant for others around the smoker. Non-smokers find it irritating to breathe "second-hand" smoke which clouds a room.

6. Smoking sets a very bad example for others. People who look up to the person who smokes, may imitate his smoking. This is especially true of children.

7. Smokers tend to come from families where parents were smokers. Children who do not smoke are often from families where parents did not smoke. Think about this, parent!

8. Smoking does not give a clean personal appearance. Often fingers are yellow and stained. Smokers have to work harder to "cover up" bad breath. Tobacco manufacturers spend millions to make a dirty habit look glamorous! But it is still a dirty habit!

Is It Right For a Christian to Smoke?

Ask yourself the following questions. Would Jesus Christ have "enjoyed a cigarette" at the Last Supper as He explained the sacrifice He was about to make on Calvary? Would He have asked for a "filter tip" when He went to pray in Gethsemane? Or would He have had a last smoke before He was nailed to the cross? Would it seem quite right to smoke as you tell a person about Jesus and as you ask that person to give his life to Him? Would it seem right to have ash trays in church and smoke during the service? Is there any way which smoking can bring honor to God? Is there any way which smoking can help you or those about you?

How Can a Person Stop Smoking?

The best way to stop smoking is never to start. But if a person has started, he can stop if he really works at it. If a person is a Christian, he has added help to give him victory.

Where Can I Get Additional Literature About Smoking?

U.S. Government Printing Office
Superintendent of Documents
Washington, D.C. 20402

National Clearinghouse for Smoking and Health
U.S. Department of Health, Education, and Welfare
Public Health Service
Health Services and Mental Health Administration
Arlington, Va. 22203

The National Congress of Parents and Teachers
700 North Rush Street
Chicago, Illinois 60611

The American Cancer Society, Inc.
219 East 42nd Street
New York, N.Y. 10017

Public Health Service
Your state capital
Your state

National Congress of Parents and Teachers
700 North Rush St.
Chicago, Illinois 60611

Questions
About Sex

EVERY CHILD IS CURIOUS. That's the way God made him. He wants to know all about the world in which he lives. He wants to know about himself, too. He may ask questions which embarrass you. But if you don't answer them to his satisfaction, he may ask others. You may not like the answers others give.

Part of the role of a parent is to educate his child. Your child *will* learn about sex somewhere. You may avoid his questions, but he will not be content with that. You may give him foolish answers, such as "the stork brought you." But when he finds that you did not tell him the truth, he will not trust some of your other answers.

Where do you expect your child to learn about sex? You must answer that question at some point in your child's growth. Where do you expect him to learn about the sanctity of sex? If not from you, where? Does your church teach it? If you don't teach it and your church doesn't teach it, your child may never hear that point of view.

There are many books today about answers to your child's questions of sex. We are concerned with the sanctity of sex primarily on these pages. Here are some questions you should be prepared to answer.

FOR YOUNGER CHILDREN—SOME QUESTIONS

Where Do Babies Come From?

God makes a little baby grow in his mother's "tummy." Only God can cause life to grow. The baby begins there from a little seed which the father gives to the mother. For nine months, the little baby grows from this seed until exactly the right time. Then God lets him come out from the mother. This is called birth. Birth is a very special time, for that is when the child begins to live a separate life from his mother. We honor this day each year by calling it our "birthday."

Why Are Girls and Boys Different?

Because that's the way God planned it. "Male and female created He them," the Bible tells us in *Genesis 5:2*. There are some things in life for mothers to do and some things for fathers to do. A mother is a special person to a baby, for the baby grows inside the mother until it is born.

But the father has his special work, too. He earns money to keep the family fed and clothed. He leads the family in its activities. Mothers and fathers together can do many things for the family which they could not do alone. God made boys and girls different so there would be mothers and fathers when they get older.

FOR OLDER CHILDREN—WHY WAIT?

You may never have this question asked of you by your children. But it does come into the mind of many teen-agers. Why wait? Why do I need to wait until I am married to have relations with another? Here are some answers.

1. Because God made you special for someone, and someone for you. The more of yourself you give away before marriage, the less happy you will be to give of yourself to the one whom God made for you. You will find later that you will be unhappy if you know that your bride or bridegroom has already given himself to someone else. He or she will be just as unhappy to hear that you have done this.

2. Because of unwanted pregnancy. Despite all the "precautions," thousands of children are born "out of wedlock" each week. Often these children are given up by both parents for adoption. Or, in some cases, the young people feel they have to get married before they really want to get married, often forcing one or both to drop out of school and get a job they don't enjoy.

3. Because of the risk of venereal disease. Gonorrhea and syphilis are both serious diseases and are both on the increase. Just because a person looks clean does not mean that he is free of these diseases. Syphilis can create serious health problems and even cause blindness in newborn children if not treated.

4. Because the Bible teaches us to wait. *Genesis 2:24* says that a man and his wife shall be "one flesh." *I Cor. 6:13* tells of the use of the body to please God, not for fornication, which is sex outside of marriage. The right use of our bodies can bring joy to ourselves and to God. The wrong use can bring untold frustration and unhappiness.

Questions
About Many Things

YOUR CHILD HAS MANY QUESTIONS. You should try to find answers to as many as you can. If you don't know, tell him. But tell him that you'll help him find the answer. Here are some questions you may wish to be prepared to answer.

Why Does a Loving God Permit Grandpa (or Someone Else) to Suffer?

The problem of pain knows no barriers. Christians die of cancer or suffer in other ways, just as non-Christians do. Jesus and God did not promise that Christians would be exempt from the problems of the world. They did promise to give a way *through* these problems (not *around* them). Christians do miss many problems which non-Christians have because they stay away from more problems. Read *I Cor. 10:13*.

Why Does God Permit So Much Crime?

There has always been crime and violence. Ezekiel once said, "The land is full of bloody crimes, and the city is full of violence" (*Ezekiel 7:23*).

This sounds very up-to-date. There was much violence in Ezekiel's time because there was much sin in the hearts and lives of the people. That is the same reason for crime and violence today. Sinful hearts cause sinful actions. Crime and violence are the fruits of our sins, not the actions of God.

Why Does There Have to Be So Much Pollution in the World?

There doesn't *have* to be. But there is, because men are selfish. Polluters are usually people who don't care about others or who don't care about the beauty of God's world. People who throw junk into a river, or empty waste materials into a stream until it kills it are putting self- and money ahead of others. As long as there is sin in the world, there will also be selfishness. Of course, if each Christian did his part, it would help, wouldn't it?

60

Why Didn't God Answer My Prayer?

Perhaps you didn't pray for something you should have! Would you want God to answer your prayer, even if He knew that He would be giving you something that was not good for you?

God answers prayer in three ways—"yes," "no," and "wait." You may have thought that God didn't answer your prayer if He said "no" or "wait." Don't think that God has to answer "yes" to every prayer. He doesn't, and won't.

Why Don't Mother and Father Live Together Anymore?

The problem of divorce is now touching one of every three homes in America. Divorce really begins in a weak system of dating. Too many young people never try to understand each other before they are married. They spend their dating time watching movies, listening to records, or some other type of "spectator" activity.

Too few young couples pray together or read the Bible together before they are married. Too few talk together about issues which may divide them later.

Becoming a Christian does not prevent divorce today because there are so many Christian couples entering into divorce. One attorney in Chicago specializes in "Christian divorces," that is, divorces among Christian couples. Perhaps too many Christian couples have not yet experienced the principle, "The family that prays together stays together."

In many cases, prayer could work out problems which could not be solved otherwise. A family founded on prayer and nurtured on prayer certainly will have less likelihood of breaking up than a prayerless family!

Why Do There Have to Be Wars?

Wars are the result of national selfishness and greed and sin, just as smaller problems are the result of individual selfishness, greed, and sin. Jesus told us to expect wars and rumors of wars. As long as there are sinners, there will be sin.

As long as there are nations which become greedy for power, there will be wars. God does not stop wars any more than He stops any other kind of sin. He lets sin continue until the end of time. Then He will separate His own from the world.

Why Didn't God Help Our Team Win?

Perhaps He did! We play in sports events to win, of course. But should we ask God to favor our team? What if there are Christians on the other team? They may be praying for the same thing. Why should we ask God to take sides?

Would that be fair for us to ask such a thing? What should we pray for when we have a sports event? First, we should pray that God will help us do our best. Some teams lose because they are lazy or aren't really trying. They deserve to lose. Second, we should pray that God will teach us good sportsmanship, and help us show good sportsmanship to others, whether we win or lose!

Why Did God Send That Tornado That Killed Some People?

God allows some things to happen, although He may not have "sent" the tornado. God has set up some beautiful forces in His world. Some of these forces are for our good—such as the rain and sunshine. Some help us to understand the power and majesty of God.

Storms teach us awe. They show us that God has great power, the power over life and death. They also teach us to respect God's power and stay out of the way of storms and floods if we can. These are important lessons to learn.

Why Does God Let Us Be Poor and Others Be Rich?

Should we ask God to make us rich? God never intended prayer for personal gain. If we could pray to be rich, everyone would be praying. Prayer empties ourselves before God. It humbles us before God, so that we can serve Him. Poverty is a problem which we must face—with God's help. It is not a problem we can dump on God. Nor can we blame Him for it.

If we are poorer than our neighbors, we should strive to make ourselves richer (if we really need more) and ask God to give us the wisdom and strength to do our best. If we truly trust Him, He will help, too. But remember! Our greatest riches are not money.

Why Didn't God Make Me Better Looking?

"Man looketh on the outward appearance; but the Lord looketh on the heart," the Bible tells us (*I Sam. 16:7*). Some "beautiful" people become proud and we don't think they're so pretty after all. Others become very beautiful by the things they do.

A Guide

***

to Character
Building

A Guide to Character Building

Success or Failure?

SUCCESS IS NOT AN ACCIDENT. It is the result of careful plans and hard work. Success is the child of dedication. It is the by-product of purposefulness.

Many parents today are frightened by the news headlines. Hardly a day goes by without some news of teens in trouble. What happened? Did these young people "go bad" in their teen years? Or are their failures the lack of concern which their parents have shown during the years since they were little children.

A child's life is a building project. The parent is the builder. He is following the Master Architect's plans in building a life—or he is failing to follow those plans. A life built on God's plans cannot fail. The only path it can follow leads to success, for God's plans do not include failure.

If you want your child to have a successful life, and who doesn't, you must work carefully to build with the building blocks of character. God has provided these building blocks in His Word, the Bible. It's up to you to use them.

Remember, though, you cannot build a building without a foundation. Before you can start to lay up these building blocks of character, you must be sure you have laid a foundation which will not crumble or fall.

Some people try to build a life on morality. This is good, but not enough. Others try to build a life on good education. We want our children to have a good education, but this is not enough. Others seek to help their children have the finest job security. That is worthwhile, too. But it is not enough.

The Bible tells us that there is one foundation alone, safe enough on which to build a life. "Other foundation can no man lay than that which is laid, which is Jesus Christ," I Corinthians 3:11 tells us. Before you begin to build with the following building blocks, help your child to give his life to Jesus Christ so that Christ will become his Savior and Lord. Then he will be able to say with Paul the Apostle, "I can do all things in Christ who strengthens me" (Philippians 4:13).

64

The Twelve Building Blocks

The twelve building blocks of character are given below. Related topics are given with each.

1. CONVICTION

Assurance, belief, faith, trust, certainty, repentance, confidence

2. DEDICATION

Consecration, devotion, offering, sanctification, commitment, discipleship, obedience, stewardship

3. REVERENCE

Respect, prayerfulness, adoration, worship, awe, honor, devotion

4. KINDNESS

Love, goodness, gentleness, unselfishness, helpfulness, generosity, grace, benevolence

5. HONESTY

Truthfulness, doing right, fairness, faithfulness, justice, sincerity, honor, uprightness

6. SELF-CONTROL

Patience, confidence, initiative, resourcefulness, responsibility, restraint, temperance, self-sacrifice

7. COURAGE

Bravery, fearlessness, heroism, valor, decision, strength

8. HUMILITY

Meekness, modesty, lowliness

9. GRATITUDE

Thankfulness, praise, loyalty, devotion

10. FRIENDLINESS

Fellowship, cooperation, enthusiasm, joyousness, acceptance

11. COMPASSION

Concern, forgiveness, sympathy, tenderness, mercy, pity

12. PERSEVERANCE

Purposefulness, determination, firmness, steadfastness, persistence

Conviction

What It Means

CONVICTION is an assurance or confidence in something or someone. In the Bible, conviction means an assurance or confidence in God and His Son, Jesus Christ.

The man of conviction trusts God completely. He *knows* that God is real, that He is with him. He *knows* that he has turned from sin and placed his trust in Jesus Christ, receiving the new life which He has offered. Faith is conviction. It is sometimes carelessly used to mean faith in anything.

But the Bible is clear in its teaching about faith or conviction. The central theme of the Bible is the salvation which is offered through faith in Jesus Christ.

Bible Stories That Teach Conviction

Noah trusted God and built the ark, v. 2, 28-35
Abraham trusted God to prevent his sacrificing Isaac, v. 2, 97-103
Joseph trusted God, even when he was a slave, v. 2, 154-157
Moses trusted God to help him lead his people from Egypt, v. 3, 48-55
Joshua trusted God to help him defeat Jericho, v. 3, 130-136
Gideon trusted God to help his three hundred defeat an army, v. 3, 144-151
David trusted God to help him defeat Goliath, v. 4, 56-63
Solomon trusted God to give him wisdom, v. 4, 166-171
Elijah trusted God to burn the sacrifice, v. 5, 33, 39
Elisha trusted God to cure Naaman, v. 5, 52-59
Daniel trusted God to keep him safe in the lions' den, v. 5, 142-149
The nobleman trusted Jesus to heal his son, v. 6, 118-123
Blind Bartimaeus trusted Jesus to give him sight, v. 8, 8-13
Peter trusted God to help him heal a lame man, v. 8, 166-171
Paul and Silas trusted God in the Philippian jail, v. 9, 106-113

Questions to Ask

1. Do I know with complete assurance that I belong to Christ, that I have given myself to Him? If not, I will ask Him now to be my Savior.
2. Do I trust God and His Son completely to guide me in my Christian life? These great men of the Bible did. Then I should, too.

Dedication

What It Means

DEDICATION is giving ourselves fully to something or someone. In the Bible, dedication means to give ourselves fully to follow the Lord Jesus Christ.

Conviction comes first, for without the full conviction that we belong to Him, we have no desire to follow Him fully.

Dedication means to set ourselves apart for the Savior's use. In that way we are sanctified, as were the holy vessels in the Temple and Tabernacle.

We belong to God and we offer our lives to do His will by being good disciples of His Son. Dedication is not only a decision, but also a daily walk.

Bible Stories That Teach Dedication

Mary dedicated her body to God for the birth of Christ, v. 6, 14-19

Wise Men dedicated their treasure to Christ, v. 6, 46-53

The first disciples dedicated their time to Christ to follow Him, v. 6, 86-91

Matthew dedicated his life to Christ to follow Him, v. 6, 152-157

Peter dedicated his beliefs to Christ as the Lord, v. 7, 58-63

The rich young ruler would not dedicate his money to Christ, v. 7, 178-183

Zacchaeus dedicated his life to Christ to follow Him, v. 8, 14-19

Mary dedicated her ointment to Christ to honor Him, v. 8, 48-53

Christ asked Peter to dedicate himself to His work, v. 8, 144-148

The disciples dedicated themselves to prayer and the Holy Spirit in the Upper Room, v. 8, 154-159

The seven deacons dedicated themselves to serving, v. 8, 186-191

Saul dedicated his life to Christ, v. 9, 31-37

Aeneas dedicated his time to tell the Gospel, v. 9, 50-55

Paul dedicated his life as a prisoner to sharing the Gospel, v. 9, 176-181

Questions to Ask

1. Will I go ANYWHERE that Jesus wants me to go?
2. Will I go cheerfully?
3. Is my mind, heart, body and soul given completely to Him?

Reverence

What It Means

REVERENCE is a deep respect for someone. It means to show great honor to that person. Reverence for God is taught in the Bible. When we revere Him, we honor Him, we adore Him, and we worship Him. Reverence for God is the highest honor we can pay. We are to honor parents, respect persons older than ourselves, but we are to worship God. Reverence means to give praise and glory to God because He is worthy of praise and glory.

How can we show reverence to God? We can pray. When we pray, let's remember to thank God for what He has given. Let's also remember to tell God how great He is and how much we love Him. Let's tell God that we want Him to guide our lives. We can also praise Him by singing and telling others about Him. We can honor God with our gifts. We can honor Him by living the kind of lives He wants us to live. But most of all, we can honor Him by giving our lives to Him so that we may be His disciples.

BIBLE STORIES THAT TEACH REVERENCE

Abel honored God by giving Him an offering, v. 2, 22-27
Noah honored God by doing what God had said, v. 2, 28-35
Joseph honored God even when he was a slave, v. 2, 154-157
David honored God by moving the ark to Jerusalem, v. 4, 120-125
Solomon honored God by asking for wisdom, v. 4, 166-171
Daniel honored God by praying, v. 5, 142-149
Mary honored God by becoming Jesus' mother, v. 6, 14-19
Peter honored God by preaching, v. 8, 160-165
Paul honored God by becoming a missionary, v. 9, 76-81

QUESTIONS TO ASK

1. Do I honor God by praying each day?
2. Do I honor God by reading my Bible each day?
3. Do I honor God by going to His house?
4. Do I honor God by telling others about Him?

68

Kindness

What It Means

KINDNESS is giving ourselves away. Kindness gives up something for the benefit of another. It is unselfishness, never selfishness. It is generosity, never greed.

It is helpfulness, never hindrance. It is love, never hate. It is tender-hearted, never hard-hearted.

Kindness is practicing the Golden Rule. How would we like for others to treat us? That's the way we should treat others. We never give to others because we think they will give something in return. That is selfishness. We give to others because that's what we would want if we were one of "the others."

The greatest kindness is to those who cannot repay. The reward of kindness is being kind, not being repaid.

BIBLE STORIES THAT TEACH KINDNESS

Abram was kind to Lot, v. 2, 68-73
Rebekah was kind to Eliezer, v. 2, 104-109
Isaac was kind to the Philistines, v. 2, 116-121
Joseph was kind to his brothers, v. 2, 172-179
Ruth was kind to Naomi, v. 3, 170-175
A family was kind to Elisha, v. 5, 46-51
Hosea was kind to his wife, v. 5, 80-85
Ebed-melech was kind to Jeremiah, v. 5, 106-111
The Good Samaritan was kind, v. 7, 98-103
The seven deacons were kind, v. 8, 186-191
Barnabas was kind to Saul, v. 9, 44-49

QUESTIONS TO ASK

1. Do I show kindness to my parents?
2. Do I give to others without expecting something back?
3. Do I help others who do not love me?
4. Do I show kindness to my brothers and sisters?

Honesty

What It Means

To be honest is to measure up to what we should be. Truthfulness is honesty of words. Purity is honesty of soul. Rightness is honesty of conduct.

An honest person is not a surprise to others. He lives according to the "yardstick" of life which God has given in His Word. He "measures up" to God's standards, which men have adopted as the standards of rightness.

To be honest is to be trustworthy. People can trust their money, their time, or their lives in the hands of an honest person. People know that an honest person will do what he says, for his hands and feet follow the same measure as his lips.

A Christian must be honest, for he walks in the steps of the perfect Son of God. The sinner has not yet faced the greatest test of honesty, to weigh himself in God's balances and seek the only One who can correct his deficiency, God's Son, Jesus Christ.

BIBLE STORIES THAT TEACH HONESTY

Abram lied to Pharaoh and almost lost his wife, v. 2, 62-67
Jacob lied to his father and almost broke up his family, v. 2, 122-127
Joseph was honest with his master and became governor, v. 2, 154-164
God gave Moses a law about honesty, v. 3, 83-89
Zacchaeus learned to be honest when he met Jesus, v. 8, 14-19
The servants with talents learned about honesty, v. 8, 40-47
Peter lied about Jesus and almost broke his heart, v. 8, 74-79
The leaders lied about Jesus and sent Him to the cross, v. 8, 80-105
Ananias and Sapphira lied and lost their lives, v. 8, 172-177

QUESTIONS TO ASK

1. Do I tell the truth even when I know it will hurt me?
2. Is there anyone who doesn't trust me? Why? How can I change this?
3. Do my words and actions always measure up the same?

70

Self-Control

What It Means

SELF-CONTROL is to control ourselves. Some people let their emotions control them. Others let their physical bodies demand certain things and control their lives. The alcoholic loses control of himself when his mind and body team up against him and demand more alcohol. The habitual smoker loses control of himself as his body and mind demand more tobacco. So does the drug addict.

We lose control of ourselves in other ways, too. Some people can't stop drinking coffee. Others have to eat candy or certain foods. Others have a compulsion to gossip or talk or complain. Others cannot make themselves do the work they know they must do.

Self-control is temperance, patience and responsibility. It makes people get started on important things when others can't move. It inspires confidence in a person when others are insecure.

Self-control is very difficult when we try to do it alone. But when we let God control our wills, our hearts, our minds, our purposes, He will give us the wisdom and help for us to control our lives.

BIBLE STORIES THAT TEACH SELF-CONTROL

Cain lost control of his emotions and killed Abel, v. 2, 22-27
Abraham controlled his fears and won God's favor, v. 2, 97-103
Isaac controlled his anger and won Philistine friends, v. 2, 116-121
Samson lost control of himself and was blinded, v. 3, 158-165
Saul lost his patience and his kingdom, v. 4, 19-24
Naaman overcame his anger and was healed, v. 5, 52-59
The rich fool died with his greed and his money, v. 7, 116-119
Pilate lost his courage and condemned Jesus to die, v. 8, 88-95

QUESTIONS TO ASK

1. How often do I get angry and want to "get even?"
2. How often do I lose my patience and want to "run ahead?"
3. Do I talk too much, or eat too much, or keep too much?

Courage

What It Means

COURAGE is a strength of mind which helps us face danger without fear. It helps us encounter difficulties with the assurance that we will overcome them. Heroes are made of courage. So are the quiet heroes who bravely suffer alone, facing difficulties known only to themselves.

Courage is boldness. While those with faint hearts sit back, men of courage move ahead, confident of victory.

The Christian is expected to be a man of courage. He must have firmness of convictions, sure that God is with him. He must face all the forces of evil which attack daily, not willing to give in to one of them. He must be willing to suffer quietly and alone, if called to do it in the name of Christ. He must also have the boldness to take the Good News to hostile people or to those who do not welcome the messenger.

A courageous Christian walks in the steps of heroes, for Jesus Christ and His apostles were examples of courage.

BIBLE STORIES THAT TEACH COURAGE

Noah built the ark while his neighbors laughed, v. 2, 28-35
Abraham was brave enough to obey God, even to give up his son, v. 2, 97-103
Joseph had the courage to do right, even in prison, v. 2, 154-157
Gideon faced an army with only three hundred men, v. 3, 144-151
David fought a giant when no one else would, v. 4, 56-63
Elijah defied four hundred enemy priests, v. 5, 40-45
Daniel faced a den of lions, v. 5, 142-149
Jesus faced the cross alone, v. 8, 96-105
Stephen faced death unafraid, v. 9, 8-13

QUESTIONS TO ASK

1. Do I ever want to "run away" from my problems?
2. Am I afraid to pray before my friends?
3. Do I have the courage to tell others about Jesus?

72

Humility

What It Means

HUMILITY is to put ourselves in our right places. Too often we want to think more highly of ourselves than we ought to think. This is pride. To think less of ourselves than we ought to think is self-destruction.

The best definition of humility for the Christian is summarized in the acrostic, JOY— Jesus first, others second, yourself last. Jesus said almost the same thing when He quoted His two favorite Scripture verses. "Love God with all your heart, soul, mind, and strength," He said. "Love your neighbor as yourself" (Mark 12:30, 31).

A humble person is meek and modest. He is not "puffed up" about his achievements. He is not a proud person. He does not brag or boast. He does not try to push himself ahead of others. But most of all, he recognizes that God is great and he is small.

BIBLE STORIES THAT TEACH HUMILITY

Rebekah watered Eliezer's camels at the well, v. 2, 104-109
Isaac let the Philistines take his wells, v. 2, 116-121
Jacob humbled himself to his brother, Esau, v. 2, 140-146
Barak humbled himself to Deborah and Jael, v. 3, 137-143
Naaman humbled himself to Elisha to be cured, v. 5, 52-59
Job was humbled before God, v. 5, 162-171
Mary humbled herself to God to become Jesus' mother, v. 6, 14-19
Shepherds humbled themselves before baby Jesus, v. 6, 32-39
Wise Men humbled themselves before young Jesus, v. 6, 46-53
Jesus spoke about humility, as that of a child, v. 7, 70-75
The prodigal son humbled himself to come home, v. 7, 140-147

QUESTIONS TO ASK

1. Do I ever brag to my friends?
2. Who's first in my life—self, others, or Jesus? Who's second?
3. Do I humble myself before God in prayer and worship?
4. Am I willing for God to use my life as He wants to use it?

Gratitude

What It Means

A GRATEFUL PERSON is a thankful person. He appreciates what someone has done for him and is willing to say so. A grateful person realizes that he is in debt to another because that person has performed some service for him or has given some gift to him.

Gratitude to God is shown by praise and thanksgiving. Many Psalms are psalms of thanksgiving, praising God for all He has done.

A grateful heart recognizes a giver and a receiver. It acknowledges a gift of worth. It is glad for the gift and for the giver.

Men have much for which they should thank God. They should thank Him for all that He has given in food and clothing and homes, and all the luxuries of life. But the Christian has even more, for "God so loved that He gave His only Son" (John 3:16). How thankful the Christian should be for everlasting life and all the wonderful benefits which come with it.

BIBLE STORIES THAT TEACH GRATITUDE

Noah was grateful when the flood ended, v. 2, 36-41
Moses was grateful when God helped at the Red Sea, v. 3, 48-55
David was grateful for God's promises, v. 4, 126-131
Naaman was grateful when God healed him, v. 5, 52-59
The shepherds were grateful for the Savior, v. 6, 32-37
Anna and Simeon were grateful for the Savior, v. 6, 40-45
One leper was grateful for Jesus' healing, v. 7, 162-167
Aeneas was grateful that Peter healed him, v. 9, 50-55
Dorcas was grateful that Peter helped her, v. 9, 56-61
Lydia was grateful that Paul brought the Gospel, v. 9, 100-105

QUESTIONS TO ASK

1. Do you ever thank God for your food at mealtime?
2. Do you thank your parents for what they do for you?
3. Do you remember to thank friends who help you?
4. Do you thank your teachers and leaders who help you?

74

Friendliness

What It Means

A FRIENDLY PERSON is someone with an outstretched hand. He wants to accept and be accepted by another. He extends his affection and hopes that others will return theirs. A friendly person is a good neighbor. He is willing to help when help is needed. He cooperates with those about him.

Friendliness is a happy experience. There is no such a thing as a sad friendship. Friendship is catching. It is infectious. It is hard to be around a friendly person and remain unfriendly. The saying is true, "If you want friends, you must be friendly."

The heart of friendliness is love. "A true friend loves at all times," Proverbs 17:17 tells us. It also says, "A brother is born for adversity." That means a friend is still a friend when trouble comes. The test of friendship comes when a friend gets into trouble and needs you. If you are a true friend, you are there to help.

BIBLE STORIES THAT TEACH FRIENDLINESS

Rebekah was friendly to Eliezer, v. 2, 104-109
Isaac was friendly to the Philistines, v. 2, 116-121
Jacob made friends with Esau, v. 2, 140-146
David and Jonathan became good friends, v. 4, 64-69
David was friendly to Mephibosheth, v. 4, 137-140
The Shunammite couple was friendly to Elisha, v. 5, 46-51
Ebed-melech was friendly to Jeremiah, v. 5, 106-111
Mary and Elizabeth were good friends, v. 6, 20-25
Mary and Martha were friends of Jesus, v. 7, 104-109
Barnabas was a true friend of Saul, v. 9, 44-49

QUESTIONS TO ASK

1. How do I choose my friends? Those who have most? Those who need me most? Do I choose friends to help me, or friends I can help?
2. Am I friendly with my own family? Do I help them?
3. Am I a good friend at ALL times? Or am I a "fair weather" friend?

Compassion

What It Means

COMPASSION is tenderness toward someone in need. It is pity for someone in trouble, charity for someone who is poor, and generosity for someone in want. Compassion reaches down and out. It offers gentleness when someone has been abused, sympathy when someone is in grief, and forgiveness when someone has sinned.

Compassion is concern for the less fortunate. It is leniency for someone in debt to us. It is grace to someone who has worked against us.

Compassion is the height of human expression, but the beginning of Divine mercy. For man it is something so demanding that it is almost beyond reach. For God it is something so basic that you cannot think of God without it.

Compassion is love that is not afraid to go anywhere to do anything for anyone. God's compassion sent Jesus to the cross to die for you and me. Our compassion should send us to the limits of our world to share the Gospel with those unfortunate ones who have never heard.

BIBLE STORIES THAT TEACH COMPASSION

Abraham showed compassion to rescue Lot, v. 2, 74-79
Abraham showed compassion to pray for Sodom, v. 2, 91-96
Joseph showed compassion to forgive his brothers, v. 2, 172-179
David showed compassion to Mephibosheth, v. 4, 137-140
Hosea showed compassion to his wife, v. 5, 80-85
Ebed-melech showed compassion to Jeremiah, v. 5, 106-111
Mary showed compassion to Jesus, v. 8, 48-53
Jesus showed compassion to the thief on the cross, v. 8, 97-102

QUESTIONS TO ASK

1. Have I helped someone in need lately? Who? What did I do?
2. Do I know someone who needs help now? What could I do?
3. Have I told someone about Jesus? Who should I tell now?
4. Have I showed compassion to others as God has to me?

Perseverance

What It Means

PERSEVERANCE may be called "keeping on keeping on." Or it may be called "stick-to-itiveness." When others quit, the man of perseverance goes on.

There's a reason for keeping on. The man of perseverance has a purpose. He knows where he is going and why. He is not willing for anything to sidetrack him until he reaches his goal.

The Christian should be the most glowing example of perseverance. He has the most clear-cut goal of all—to follow Jesus Christ. He has the most help of all—the Holy Spirit by his side. He has the greatest reward of all—the crown of righteousness.

Perseverance is steadfastness, persistence, constancy, resolve, zeal and devotion. The man of perseverance is a man of decision. He has set his ambitions and will not move from them because he is confident that they are right.

Persevere for Jesus! That is what Paul said in Philippians 3:12-16. Once you set your eyes on this heavenly goal, you will never quit!

BIBLE STORIES THAT TEACH PERSEVERANCE

Noah kept on building the ark for many years, v. 2, 28-35
Abraham waited for years for God's promise, v. 2, 80-84
Joseph kept on being faithful to God, even in trouble, v. 2, 147-164
Moses kept on following God's orders, v. 3, 36-47
Daniel kept on praying, even in danger, v. 5, 142-149
The midnight bread borrower kept on knocking, v. 7, 110-115
The disciples kept on praying in the upper room, v. 8, 154-159

QUESTIONS TO ASK

1. How often do I want to quit? Is my project worthwhile?
2. What is my greatest goal in life? Will I feel like quitting it?
3. Have I set my highest purpose to work for Jesus?
4. Do I pray daily, asking God to help me keep on with my work?

How to Build
These Important Building Blocks
Into Your Child's Life

HERE ARE suggestions to help you build these important building blocks into your child's life.

1. Set a Good Example

What your child sees you do, he may imitate. Build his life by setting a good example.

2. Show Him Other Good Examples

Help him see these building blocks in the lives of great people. Heroes' lives are usually built with these same characteristics.

3. Teach Him What God Says About Them

The Bible is filled with the words and thoughts which God has given concerning these important building blocks. Teach him what God says and help him understand what this means to him.

4. Provide Experiences Where He Can Learn Them

Many of these important truths are learned by practice. Encourage him to have experiences where he can learn these important truths by putting them into his own life.

5. Encourage Him and Pray For Him

The child needs most of all for you to encourage him and pray for him. He needs to know that you're "on his side" hoping that he will succeed. Don't try to nag him into success. Make these things so exciting and desirable that he will *want* them.

78

A Guide

to Great Bible Truths

A Guide to Great Bible Truths

What Is Truth?

PILATE ASKED that question when he judged Jesus (John 18:38). If only Pilate had known that *Truth* stood before him, about to be condemned by the lies of the crowd.

Jesus said, "I am the way, the *Truth,* and the life (John 14:6). He also said that the Holy Spirit is *Truth* (John 14:17), and that God the Father is *Truth* (John 3:33). We read also that the Word of God is *Truth* (Psalm 119:160 and John 17:17).

Truth Is Changeless

Lies wear many faces, but truth stands unchanged forever. It is a standard which never varies, a treasure which never rots, rusts, or fades. Truth is beauty which never grows old or dies.

But the world about us seems to offer no perfect measures, no changeless beauty, nothing safe from rot or decay.

Men are born, rise to greatness, and set forth signs of power. They build empires and utter wise words. We are tempted to trust in them and their works.

But men's minds change. Their empires crumble. The words spoken for one generation may be despised by the next. The captains and the kings grow old and die and their successors struggle to erase their marks of greatness or to surpass them. So man and his message is like a flower, pleasant for a short time, but too transcient to trust forever.

Nature itself is transcient. It constantly changes. Nothing stands still. Nothing keeps its face unchanged forever.

Truth Is Perfect

Where can we find something or someone so reliable that we can hitch our destinies to perfection? Where can we put our futures on a "sure thing," something which cannot fail? Where can we find truth so perfect that it will never let us down, even when we die?

80

Where Is Truth?

WE HAVE ALREADY READ where we can find truth. God is true. His Son, His Holy Spirit, His Word, His judgments are true.

God is the measure of perfectness which will never change—throughout all time and on through the endless ages of eternity. Whatever is perfect is like God.

Trust in men and empires and they will crumble into dust, only to be excavated and analyzed by tomorrow's archaeologists. Trust in nature and it will wither and die or be destroyed by the carelessness of man himself.

Trust in self alone and your god will face his greatest failure in the mirror. When self fails where can one go for help?

Nobody but God, nothing but God, is absolutely true. God and His Son and His Holy Spirit are the same, and they remain unchanged, yesterday, today, and forever" (Hebrews 13:8).

Where Do We Learn God's Truth?

Where do we learn about the truth of God? In the timeless truths of His Word, the Bible.

God has given us a record of His negotiations with men. He has spoken through men of old and has inspired them to write His message to us and to all men. He has breathed the breath of truth on His chosen messengers and they have written it for us to read. When God has done this for us, we should take the time to read it.

Since our source of truth is the Bible, we need to learn all we can about it. We need to study it and put its timeless message to work in our lives.

The Great Truths

The following pages seek to simplify the great truths of the Bible so that we may more easily make them a part of our daily lives. The truth of God is not merely to be learned. It must be lived.

It must not end with our heads. It must find its way into our hands and feet and lips.

Then someone may say of us the words which John the Apostle wrote, "I greatly rejoiced when someone told me about the truth of your life, for you certainly do follow the truth" (III John 3). Truth brings joy to us and to others.

The Truth About God

THE BIBLE IS GOD'S BOOK. It was written by God. It was written about God. There are many important truths about God in it. Here are some questions which the Bible answers.

Is There a God?

Atheists Say No

Some people say there is no God. They are called atheists. Some live as though there is no God. They are atheists too, even though they may not like the word.

The Bible tells about atheists in Psalm 14:1. It says, "The fool says in his heart that there is no God." This is what God thinks of atheists. Would you want God to say this about you?

The Bible Says Yes

The Bible begins with God. "In the beginning, God created" is the opening statement of the Bible (Genesis 1:1).

God is the central person throughout the Bible. His name is mentioned about four thousand times in the Bible. The Bible ends with God and a warning not to add to His Word. To believe in the Bible is to believe in God.

Millions of People Say Yes

If you believe in God, you are not alone. Millions throughout all ages believed also. How could so many people be so wrong for so many centuries?

The World About Us Says Yes

Everything that is made had to have a maker. Someone had to build the house you live in, the car you ride in, the clothing you wear. Nothing "just happens."

The world is a beautiful, carefully designed instrument. The times and seasons show a lovely plan.

The snowflakes are works of art. The flowers are masterpieces of beauty. The careful design of the universe speaks to each of us about a Master Designer, God.

Who Is God?

God Is a Spirit

How do we know that God is a spirit? Because Jesus said so, and Jesus had lived with God.

When Jesus talked with the woman at the well, He said, "God is a spirit. Those who worship Him must worship in spirit and truth" (John 4:24). Jesus ought to know!

What is a spirit? In Luke 24:39 we read, "A spirit does not have flesh and bones." A spirit does not have a physical body such as ours. It has a special body, but it is not flesh and blood.

A spirit is invisible (Colossians 1:15). It is "incorruptible," that is, not subject to disease, old age, or death, as our physical bodies are.

God Is a Person

Although God is invisible, without a body such as the kind we have, He is a real person. He has a mind and can think. He has intelligence and can show wisdom.

God loves, hates, plans, works, reasons, shows jealousy, grieves, and does other things which we see people do (see Rev. 3:19; Prov. 6:16; Deut. 6:15; I Kings 11:9; and Gen. 6:6). Man was made in the image of God, so God and man have similar kinds of personality. The characteristics which describe God are the same which describe man, except for those distinct characteristics mentioned on these pages. The things which make us a "person" can be seen in God also, for we have been made to be like Him.

God Is One Person,
Who Has Shown Himself in Three Ways

The Bible teaches that God is one person (Deut. 6:4; I Tim. 2:5; and I Cor. 8:4). But God has shown Himself in three ways, as Father, Son, and Holy Spirit, three different ways of presenting Himself to men. See Romans 1:7 (Father); Hebrews 1:8 (Son); and Acts 5:3, 4 (Holy Spirit).

This is a difficult truth to understand and many have tried different ways of explaining it. Like many truths in the Bible, our human minds are not big enough to grasp it. But we are to accept it because it is true, because the Bible says it is.

What Is God Like?

God Knows Everything

God knows all that is happening in the world. Nothing takes place without the eyes of God watching it (Prov. 15:3; Prov. 5:21; Psalm 147:4; Psalm 147:5; I John 3:20; Romans 11:33). All that happens to people is known and watched by God. He sees everything that every person is doing (Exod. 3:7; Prov. 5:21; Psalm 139:2-4). God even knows the number of hairs in each person's head (Matt. 10:29, 30).

God knows everything you do, whether you do it in public or in secret. He sees you in the quietness of your room or in the busy crowd on a city street. He knows and He cares. He knows when you have the smallest problem or the greatest crisis. He wants to help you, if you will ask Him.

God Can Do Everything

God has the power to do anything He wants to do. There is nothing which He cannot do. God made the world and the heavens around it (Gen. 1:1-3). He can shake mountains (Nahum 1:5, 6) and control the storm (Psalm 107:25-29). God controls the angels (Dan. 4:35; Heb. 1:14) and even limits the power of Satan (Job 1:12; 2:6).

God can do whatever He wants to do in your life. But God does not force you to do anything. He will lead you and guide you. But as a God of love, He lets you move within His will and His way. God can give you great power to do mighty things for Him if you will ask Him. He can do in you more than you ever dreamed.

God Is Everywhere

There is no place in all the world where God is not present at all times. Man can find no hiding place from God (Psalm 139:7-12). God is in the highest heavens (Job 22:12-14). He is nearby at any time (Jer. 23:23, 24). He is never absent from us, for in Him we live, and move, and exist (Acts 17:24-28).

Even though God's presence is everywhere, He has special places where He lives. Heaven is His home (I Kings 8:30; Rev. 21:2; Isaiah 66:1). God went with the Children of Israel in a cloud and fire, and "dwelt" at the Tabernacle, and later at the Temple. Perhaps it could be said that God lives in Heaven but extends Himself through all creation.

84

God Lives Forever

God has lived and will live forever. There was never a time when God did not live. There will never be a time when He does not live (Hab. 1:12; Psalm 90:2; 102:24-27; Exod. 3:14; Rev. 1:8). Through all the ages of the past, present and future, God keeps on living.

God Is Perfect and Holy

God never does anything wrong. He never makes a mistake. Job said that God could not do any wickedness or evil (Job 34:10). God is holy, or pure. He cannot keep on looking at sin (Hab. 1:13). Because God is pure, He wants us to be pure, too (I Peter 1:15, 16).

God Is Faithful and True

God never lets anyone down. He never promises something that He will not do. God always tells the truth and lives by it. All He does is right (Psalm 145:17). For those who work His works, God faithfully rewards (Heb. 6:10; II Tim. 4:8).

God will never lie to you. He will never say that He will do something, then fail to do it. If there is ever any failure, it will be ours, not His.

God Is Good and Merciful

Since God is good, He wants to give His goodness to all who will receive it. God does not get angry quickly (Psalm 103:8). He wants to forgive those who seek Him (Isaiah 55:7; II Peter 3:9). God's mercy causes Him to give to those who do not deserve it.

Whatever good there is in the world has come from God. Whatever good there is in you has come from God, directly or indirectly. If you want a good life, then you should seek a godly life.

God Is Love

God loves all men and wants them to come to Him. He loves men so much, that He sent His only Son to die for them (John 3:16). Even though men are sinners, God still loves them and tries to win them to Himself.

Since God is love, His people should also show His love in their lives. If God so loved the world that He gave, then we also should so love the world that we give. Christ living in us is also Christ giving through us.

What Does God Do?

God is the author of life. He created the world and the universe. He created man. He keeps on creating life as new babies are born, new plants and animals come into the world, and new life begins around us. God takes care of His creation, providing for it and keeping it going. God also tries to win lost men back to Himself. When men return to Him, He guides them through life and prepares a home for them in Heaven.

God, through His Holy Spirit, goes with His followers, helping them live pure lives and do things that honor Him. He teaches them His way and helps them walk in it.

God works through His people. As God's people move among the people of the world, preaching, teaching, winning, praying, and urging, God works through their hands and feet and lips. Someone has said that God has no other hands but our hands, no other feet but our feet, and no other lips to speak His praise but our lips. God could work without us, but He has chosen to work through us.

God offers through His people a new life in Jesus Christ. He gives salvation and helps men live in harmony with that new life. He gives joy and peace and all other qualities which go with it.

BIBLE STORIES THAT TEACH ABOUT GOD

God is the creator, V. 2, 6-13
God provides all Adam and Eve need, V. 2, 14-21
God punishes Cain's sin, V. 2, 22-27
God keeps Noah, his faithful one, safe, V. 2, 36-41
God promises Noah and sends a rainbow, V. 2, 42-49
God makes a covenant with Abraham, V. 2, 80-84
God takes care of his faithful servant, Joseph, V. 2, 158-164
God chooses Moses for a special job, V. 3, 30-35
God punishes the disobedient Pharaoh, V. 3, 36-47
God leads His own people, V. 3, 48-55
God gives food to His hungry people, V. 3, 64-73
God gives water to His thirsty people, V. 3, 74-78
God gives good rules for His people to follow, V. 3, 83-89
God calls Samuel for special work, V. 3, 186-191
God rewards Solomon for asking for wisdom, V. 4, 172-177
God protects Daniel in the lions' den, V. 5, 142-149
God introduces His Son to the world, V. 6, 72-77

86

The Truth About Jesus Christ

JESUS CHRIST is the focal point of history. The rise and fall of nations and empires, the presence of sin and disobedience in governments and individuals pointed to one important truth. In his own strength and goodness, man could never measure up to the simple rules that God had given at Mount Sinai, rules that were necessary to show men how to please God.

Man had failed in God's simple request, "Love and obey the One who made you." So God prepared another way, through His Son, Jesus Christ.

WHO IS JESUS CHRIST?

Jesus is both God and man. He is God who came to earth to live for a few years in the body of a man. That is called His incarnation, or coming into flesh.

Jesus the man

The Bible tells us that Jesus was born of a woman, Mary (Matthew 1: 18; 2: 11; 12: 47; 13: 55). The Baby at Bethlehem had a body like that of other babies at Bethlehem and other cities of the world.

Jesus grew up like other men. He had human strength. He grew tall and wise (Luke 2: 40, 52).

Jesus looked like other men. The woman of Samaria looked upon Him as a Jew, for He probably looked Jewish in His features (John 4: 9). His face and other features did not cause the woman to think that God had sent Him. But His words and message to her did.

When Cleopas and his friend walked with Jesus on the road to Emmaus, they thought He was just another man. His features did not suggest anything special. But when they finally knew that it was Jesus, they remembered that what He had said "made their hearts burn within them," not what He had looked like (Luke 24: 32).

Jesus ate and slept and wept like any other man. After His baptism, He went into the wilderness to pray. He grew hungry (Matthew 4: 2). He was tempted, like other men (Matthew 4: 3; Hebrews 4: 15). On the cross, He became thirsty (John 19: 28). Like other men, He became tired (John 4: 6). He also slept, as other men sleep (Matthew 8: 24). When Lazarus died, Jesus cried like a man (John 11: 35). At Calvary, He died, like any other man (John 19: 30).

87

But there was one characteristic of men that Jesus did not have. Jesus never yielded to temptation. He never sinned. We know that He is the only man who never sinned (Romans 3: 23; I John 3: 5).

Jesus the Son of God

While Jesus had a body of a man, as well as all the characteristics of man except sin, He was also God. He is called God in Titus 2: 13; John 20: 28; I John 5: 20.

Jesus was God who entered the body of a baby at Bethlehem, to live in that human body until His death at Calvary. Because of the birth at Bethlehem, Jesus called Himself the Son of God. The Spirit of God had united with a virgin woman to create the only Child ever born with one human parent and one Divine parent. Jesus as the Son of God was God incarnated into human flesh, God's Spirit in a human body.

Thus, God limited Himself when He came into the body of Mary's baby. He limited Himself in time and place. As Jesus, God could only go to one place at one time. He had to eat and sleep. And He had to die. Philippians 2: 5-11 tells how God in Christ humbled Himself, even to die on the cross.

It is difficult for people to understand how God could come into a human body, as Jesus, yet still remain in Heaven as God the Father. The answer is simple, yet hard to understand. God is all powerful, all wise, and everywhere. He could do this miracle, but we cannot understand exactly how because we can think only in a limited way. Our minds are too small to understand, even if God chose to explain the method. But we are to accept the truth of it, even though we cannot understand God's method.

One important truth taught in the Bible is that Jesus was born of a virgin, a woman who had never had sexual relations before. Thus it could never be said that Jesus' birth was of a human father. God was His father. Jesus was God's Son, God in human flesh.

WHAT IS JESUS LIKE?

Jesus is the Creator

The Bible says that Jesus was there when the world was created. "All things were made by Him," we are told (John 1: 3). "In Him all things were created, in Heaven and on earth, visible and invisible . . . all things were made by Him and for Him" (Col. 1: 16). These Scriptures show that Jesus and God were the same Person, performing the same work, even though they are revealed to men in different ways. As with many of the truths of God, the method is a mystery, but the truth is a certainty to be accepted.

Jesus Is the Sustainer

It is Jesus who keeps the world together. His power controls the destiny of the world and its peoples. Like some strange magnetic force, Jesus' power holds the world together (Col. 1: 17).

The power and presence of God is not absent, living in some faraway place. It is present in every activity, holding the atoms of the universe together.

Jesus Is Forgiveness

This was the purpose of His visit to earth, to forgive sin. In Matthew 9: 6, Jesus says that He has "power on earth to forgive sins." That was the purpose of His death, to pay the penalty for sin, so it could be forgiven.

Jesus Is Eternal

Jesus has always lived. He was not born at Bethlehem, for He lived thousands of years before then. But He came into the world in a human body at Bethlehem.

Jesus said, "Before Abraham was, I Am" (John 8:58), which meant that He lived before Abraham. Speaking of Jesus, John said, "In the beginning was the Word" (John 1:1).

Jesus Is Life

Life has come from Jesus Christ. John 1: 4 says, "in Him was life." Jesus said, "I am the Way, the Truth, and the Life" (John 14: 6). Since Jesus, as God of Creation, made all things, your life and mine have come from Him.

Jesus is not only life, but He is everlasting life. Through His power, we may have a life that goes on and on forever.

Jesus said, "Whosoever liveth and believeth in Me shall never die" (John 11:26). John 17:3 also tells of Jesus, the source of eternal life, life that never ends.

Much of Jesus' ministry was spent in healing the sick, restoring life that had been ruined. Some of it was spent in raising people from the dead, or bringing them back to this life. Much of it was spent in preaching and teaching, or telling people how to live.

Jesus Is Lord and Master

Jesus is Lord of life itself. He is "King of kings, and Lord of lords" (I Timothy 6: 14, 15). There is no man in all the world, now or ever, as great as Jesus. If kings and lords are under Him, how much more Jesus' own disciples are subject to His leadership. Jesus said that He is Master and Lord (John 13: 13). God set Jesus at His right hand, far above all "principality, and power, and might, and dominion" (Ephesians 1: 20, 21).

Jesus Is All Powerful

Jesus has power over all things (Hebrews 1: 3; 2: 8). His power extends over Heaven and earth (Matthew 28: 18). He has power over life and death, health and disease, demons and hell, even over the forces of nature.

Jesus Is All Wise

All wisdom and knowledge of the earth are hidden in Jesus (Col. 2:3). He knows all that is in people (John 2:25). Jesus' disciples recognized that He knew all things (John 16:30).

Jesus Is Everywhere

When Jesus gave the Great Commission to His disciples, He told them to go into all the world with the Gospel and He would go with them. Every preacher, teacher, and missionary who gives the Gospel to others, no matter where he is, has Jesus by his side (Matthew 28: 19, 20). Jesus said, "Where two or three are gathered together in my name, there am I in the midst of them" (Matthew 18: 20). He attends every prayer meeting in the world!

WHAT WAS JESUS' WORK?

Jesus came to earth to live, to teach, to die, and to rise again. Each part of His work was most important.

Through His life, Jesus showed us how to live the way His followers should. He set the perfect example for every believer who would ever live.

Through His teachings, Jesus told us what would please God. He showed us the way of salvation and the way of life for those who accept Him. He taught about God and Heaven. The teachings of Jesus Christ give us a system of Christian truth which is essential for us to know.

Through His death Jesus redeemed, or bought back from sin, all men. He made a way to Heaven by paying the full penalty for sin. Through His blood, Jesus made an offering once and for all, a sacrifice for sin so that we might come to God through Him.

Through His resurrection, Jesus conquered death and paved a way for His followers to conquer death also. His resurrection brought hope to all men of a life after death in Heaven. It brought an assurance that all who follow Christ can have that hope.

Through His ascension into Heaven, Jesus proved that He came from Heaven. His work in Heaven is to prepare a home for His followers. His work on earth continues, for He goes with each believer in his daily walk and work. He listens to each prayer and stands between each believer and God.

BIBLE STORIES THAT TEACH ABOUT JESUS

All the stories of the New Testament teach about Jesus. Micah's prophecy (v. 5, 188-191) tells about His coming.

The Truth About the Holy Spirit

To MANY PEOPLE, the Holy Spirit is a mystery. That is because so few of us have taken the time to study what the Bible says about the Holy Spirit. Yet, the Holy Spirit is no less God than Jesus or the Father.

God the Father revealed Himself to men in the Old Testament. God the Son revealed Himself to men in New Testament times, as recorded in the Gospels. God the Holy Spirit has revealed Himself to men since Jesus left the earth at the ascension. His work is recorded in the Book of Acts and the Epistles.

WHO IS THE HOLY SPIRIT?

To many people, the Holy Spirit seems far removed from their lives. Jesus is easier to know, for many pictures have been drawn, showing Him in a human body such as the one we have. Jesus came to earth and lived among men. Much is said about Him in the Gospels. Much that He said is recorded there also.

In the Old Testament, we read much of the Father's contact with the patriarchs and the prophets, with Moses and Joshua, Samuel and David, Solomon and Elisha. He talked with these people and helped them in their work.

But the average person would probably not be able to quote a single word which the Holy Spirit spoke to people. Yet there are many places in the Bible where He did talk with men and work with them.

Because the Holy Spirit is less known to many, He seems more impersonal. Yet the Bible tells us some very specific things about Him. This is what we want to learn.

The Holy Spirit Is God

The Holy Spirit is God, just as the Father and the Son are God. These three are all one. God is one Person, but He has revealed Himself in three ways to men—as a Father, as Jesus Christ or God in flesh, and as the Holy Spirit. The Holy Spirit is God in every way.

All the characteristics of God are spoken of the Holy Spirit. He lives forever (Hebrews 9: 14), He knows everything (I Cor. 2: 10, 11), He is all-powerful (Luke 1: 35), and He is everywhere (Psalm 139: 7-10).

The Holy Spirit is mentioned equally with the Father and Son in the

Great Commission (Matthew 28:19). Jesus said we are to baptize people in the name of the Father, the Son, and the Holy Spirit.

The Holy Spirit did work which only God can do. He was the God who created the universe, just as the Father and Son also (Genesis 1:2; Psalm 104:30; Job 33:4). The re-creation which takes place in salvation is the work of the Spirit (John 3:5-8).

The Holy Spirit Has Many Names

The names of the Holy Spirit help us to understand more about Him and who He is. Some names show that the Holy Spirit and Jesus perform some tasks together. Other tasks are specifically for One or the Other. Here are some of His names.

THE SPIRIT OF TRUTH. Jesus called the Holy Spirit by this name three times (John 14:17; 15:26; 16:13). John wrote that the Holy Spirit is truth (I John 5:6).

THE SPIRIT OF WISDOM. Isaiah prophesied about Jesus, the Messiah, and the Holy Spirit who would be upon Him (Isaiah 11:2). In his prophecy, Isaiah called the Holy Spirit "the Spirit of Wisdom."

THE SPIRIT OF LIFE. Paul gave this term to the Holy Spirit (Romans 8:2). The Spirit of Life stands in contrast with the spirit of sin and death.

THE SPIRIT OF GRACE. Grace, that which we do not deserve, is given by the Holy Spirit (Hebrews 10:29). When salvation is offered to men, who do not deserve it, God the Holy Spirit is offering His grace. When men refuse it, they are insulting the Holy Spirit. There is no hope for those who refuse this wonderful offer.

SPIRIT OF PROMISE. The Holy Spirit completes the promises of God in the lives of the believers (Ephesians 1:13). All that God promised can be fulfilled if we let the Holy Spirit have His way.

SPIRIT OF COUNSEL, SPIRIT OF MIGHT, SPIRIT OF KNOWLEDGE AND THE FEAR OF THE LORD. These names are all given to the Holy Spirit by Isaiah (Isaiah 11:2) when he prophesied about the Holy Spirit coming upon Christ, the Messiah.

SPIRIT OF BURNING. The Holy Spirit is pictured in Isaiah as a Spirit which burns away guilt and sin (Isaiah 4:4). John the Baptist said that the baptism of Jesus would be with the Holy Spirit and with fire (Matthew 3:11, 12). He also was speaking of the purifying fire of the Holy Spirit.

SPIRIT OF GOD. Many times in Scriptures the Holy Spirit is mentioned as the Spirit of God (See Genesis 1:2, I Corinthians 3:16), the Spirit of the Lord (Micah 2:7; Isaiah 40:13).

THE HOLY SPIRIT. The New Testament Scriptures which refer to the Holy Spirit often call Him by that name (Romans 14: 17; I Cor. 6: 11, 19; and Titus 3: 5, 6). Some versions of the Bible translate this name as Holy Ghost.

THE SPIRIT. A number of New Testament Scriptures call Him by the name "The Spirit." But these clearly mean The Holy Spirit (Matt. 4: 4; Col. 1: 8; I Pet. 3: 18; I John 3: 24).

THE SPIRIT OF YOUR FATHER. Jesus told His disciples that the Spirit of the Father would speak in them (Matthew 10: 20). He was talking about the Holy Spirit.

THE ETERNAL SPIRIT (Heb. 9: 14), SPIRIT OF THE LORD GOD (Isaiah 61:1), SPIRIT OF THE LORD (Isaiah 63:14), SPIRIT OF THE LIVING GOD (II Cor. 3:3), SPIRIT OF HIS SON (Gal. 4:6), are other names used for the Holy Spirit.

THE COMFORTER (or THE COUNSELOR) is an important name for the Holy Spirit. Jesus used this name, saying the Holy Spirit would counsel and comfort those who are believers (John 14: 15, 25; 15: 26). The name is The Comforter in some versions. In other versions of the Bible, the name is The Counselor.

THE WORK OF THE HOLY SPIRIT

The Holy Spirit has many kinds of work. Here is a list of some of those mentioned in the Bible. Notice how many of these works involve you.

He was creator (Gen. 1:26, 27; Job 33:4)
He was author of new birth (John 3:5, 6; I John 5:4)
He raised Christ from the dead (Acts 2:24; I Pet. 3:18; Heb. 13:20; Rom. 1:4)
He inspired the writing of Scripture (II Tim. 3:16; II Pet. 1:21)
He is the source of wisdom (Isaiah 11:2; John 14:26; 16:13; I Cor. 12:8)
He is the source of miracles (Matt. 12:28; Luke 11:20; Acts 19:11; Rom. 15:19)
He appoints and sends ministers (Matt. 9:38; Acts 13:2, 4; 20:28)
He convinces of sin, righteousness, and judgment (John 16:8-11)
He dwells in saints (John 14:17; I Cor. 3:16; 6:19; 14:25)
He comforts or counsels the church (Acts 9:31; II Cor. 6:19)
He sanctifies the church (Ezek. 37:28; Rom. 15:16)
He directs the preaching of the Gospel (Acts 16:6, 7, 10)

94

He directs ministers where not to preach (Acts 16:6, 7)
He helps ministers know what to preach (I Cor. 2:13)
He struggles with sinners (Gen. 6:3)
He scolds (John 16:8)
He helps our weaknesses (Rom. 8:26)
He teaches (John 14:26; I Cor. 12:3)
He guides (John 16:13)
He glorifies Christ (John 16:14)
He searches all things (Rom. 11:33, 34; I Cor. 2:10, 11)
He lives inside the believer (I Cor. 6:19; Rom. 8:9)
He fills the believer (Acts 2:4; Eph. 5:18)

BIBLE STORIES THAT TEACH ABOUT THE HOLY SPIRIT

Visits Jesus' baptism in the form of a dove, v. 6, 72-77
Comes upon disciples in upper room, v. 8, 154-159
Begins a revival at Pentecost, v. 8, 160-165
Works among believers at Samaria, v. 9, 20-23
Leads Philip to the Ethiopian, v. 9, 24-30

The Truth About Man

THE DOCTRINE OF MAN is Bible truth about you and me. It tells us what we look like in God's eyes. It tells us what lies deep inside us and why we are what we are. To understand the Gospel, God's Good News to man, we must first understand man. To understand the plan of salvation, we must first understand the sinner who needs it.

WHAT IS MAN LIKE?

Man Is Like God in Some Ways

The Bible tells us that man is made in "the image of God" (Gen. 9: 6). That means that he is like God in some ways. He is not exactly like God, for if he were, he would be God.

But God put into man some of the characteristics of Himself. He made man an intelligent creature, with a mind to think. Man can make plans and can carry them out. Like God, he can reason, organize, follow a logical idea, and express his mind in words.

Like God, man also has the knowledge of good and evil. He can know what is right and what is wrong.

Man is a spiritual person, as God is. The real you is a spirit, living inside a body made of flesh. Man is trapped inside this body of flesh, and is not like God in that way. But his spirit is eternal, like God. His spirit will live forever, either in Heaven or in Hell.

Man Has a Will

Man is not putty in the hands of God. He can choose which way he will go. With his mind, man can know what is right or wrong. With his heart, he can want right or wrong. But with his will, he decides to do right or wrong.

The will of man can make him set himself against God. It can set his purposes in harmony with God. Through his will, man determines to follow Christ or his own passions.

Man Has a Conscience

Man has a power in him called conscience. It is a measuring stick, built inside man. It measures each thought, deed, or word by some perfect measure which has been set up. For the believer, this measure is the Word

96

of God and the Person of Christ. "To be like Him" is our measure. "To obey His Word" is another way of saying it, but it all comes out the same. If we obey His Word, we will be like Him.

Man Has a Personality

Like God, man is a person. Each man has a definite self, slightly different from that of his neighbor. He is capable of knowing and loving and sharing and working, in his own way. Whatever he does or says is somewhat different from the words and actions of others. That is what makes you what you are, but different from all other people in the world.

WHAT HAPPENED TO MAN?

The Bible teaches us that man fell, or entered into sin. By obeying the voice of Satan, rather than the voice of God, man became a sinner. Every man has followed this pattern (Romans 3:23). All have sinned and failed to measure up to the perfect yardstick of God's law, His Word, and His Son.

This is the reason for salvation. This is why Christ died, to make a way possible for the sinner to be saved, for fallen man to come back to his God.

BIBLE STORIES THAT TEACH ABOUT MAN

The creation of man, v. 2, 6-13
The fall of man, v. 2, 14-21
The punishment of man's sin, v. 2, 28-49
The atonement for man's sin, v. 8, 96-117
The evangelism of man, v. 8, 160-165

The Truth About Salvation

THE FOCAL POINT of all history was the Cross of Christ. From the Creation to the Cross, man showed himself to be a sinner, not capable of living the way God wanted. Nations and empires rose and fell, but none was patterned after God's rules.

God chose one nation among all nations. He wrote the laws for this nation, led it through a wilderness and fed it with miracle food. God helped this nation, Israel, defeat its enemies and gave it a promised land. But even though God did so much for Israel, even His chosen people could not please Him.

Weakened by sin and idol worship, the chosen people divided their nation and let foreign kings destroy them. Then Jesus came. He made a new way to God by dying on the cross and rising from the dead. His new plan was called salvation. There are other terms associated with salvation, too. This section will study those terms and what they mean.

REPENTANCE

Without repentance, salvation is not possible. An unrepentant sinner will not be received at God's place of mercy. For without repentance, the sinner is not sorry that he is a sinner. He shows his desire to keep his sin. Salvation is for those who want to have sins forgiven. It is for those who repent (Matthew 3: 2; Luke 15: 7; Acts 17: 30).

What Repentance Is

Repentance is feeling sorry for sin and having a desire to turn in the opposite direction. When a person repents, he changes both his mind and his heart.

Bible Stories That Teach Repentance

Joseph's brothers repented of their evil, v. 2, 172-179
David repented of his sin with Bathsheba, v. 4, 132-136
David repented of his sin of numbering the people, v. 4, 153-159
The prodigal son repented and went home, v. 7, 140-147
Zacchaeus repented and gave himself to Jesus, v. 8, 14-19
The people at Pentecost repented, v. 8, 160-165
The Ephesians repented and burned their evil books, v. 9, 126-131

FAITH

As repentance is turning away from something, so faith is turning toward something. When a man repents, he turns from sin. When he shows faith, he turns toward God. Without faith, we cannot please God or Jesus (Heb. 11:6).

What Faith Is

Faith is belief or complete confidence in God. It is a trust in the truth of what has been said about Him in the Bible. It is an acceptance of what may humanly be unacceptable.

The man of faith *knows* that these things are true. He *agrees* to that truth. And he accepts that truth of God personally.

Bible Stories That Teach Faith

By faith, Noah built the ark, v. 2, 28-35
By faith, Abraham went to a strange country, v. 2, 56-61
By faith, Abraham prepared to offer Isaac, v. 2, 97-103
By faith, Joseph remained true to God in Egypt, v. 2, 154-164
By faith, Moses led the people of Israel into the wilderness, v. 3, 48-55
By faith, Ruth went with Naomi to a new land, v. 3, 170-175
By faith, Blind Bartimaeus received his sight, v. 8, 8-13
By faith, Paul and Barnabas took the Gospel to other lands, v. 9, 76-81
By faith, Lydia became a believer, v. 9, 100-105
By faith, Paul trusted God to take care of him at Rome, v. 9, 158-181

THE NEW BIRTH

Salvation is not only repentance, or turning from sin, and faith, or turning to God, but it is also the new birth. Jesus told Nicodemus, "You must be born again" (John 3:3-8). Peter talked also of the new birth (I Peter 1:23) as did John (I John 3:9; 5:4).

What the New Birth Is

When each of us entered this physical world, we came by a physical birth. We were born. We entered a material place with a material body. As we came into the world, we became alive when we breathed the breath of this world into our lungs.

But when we are saved from sin, we enter the Kingdom of Heaven, which is a spiritual world. We are born again, not with a physical birth, but with a spiritual birth. As we enter this spiritual world, we breathe the Breath of God, the Holy Spirit, who enters into us, making us alive to Him and His spiritual world.

The new birth is sometimes called regeneration (Titus 3:5). The word regeneration means to give a new life. The new birth brings a new life to the believer. Old things pass away. All things become new (II Cor. 5:17).

When a man is born again, or given the new birth, he has a new nature. That is, he becomes a different kind of person.

He is created again in the likeness of God, just as Adam was in the beginning (Ephesians 4:22-24). This new nature, in the likeness or image of God, is made in holiness and righteousness (Eph. 4:24; Col. 3:10).

Bible Stories That Teach the New Birth

Nicodemus learned about the new birth from Jesus, v. 6, 104-111
Zacchaeus experienced the new birth when he came to Jesus, v. 8, 14-19
Saul was born again on the road to Damascus, v. 9, 31-37
The Philippian jailer was born again, v. 9, 106-113
King Agrippa heard about the new birth from Paul, v. 9, 152-157

JUSTIFICATION

Repentance is turning from sin. Faith is turning to God. The new birth is God re-making us spiritually, or giving us a new life with a new spirit. Justification is a new relationship to God. It tells how God looks on the new Christian.

When a man becomes a new person in Christ, God no longer looks upon him as a sinner, separated from Him. Instead, he looks upon that man as a righteous person, a person who has not sinned. This is called justification.

Someone has said that justification could be called "just-as-if-I'd-never-sinned." That's the way God looks at the person who has had his sins forgiven and has received the new life in Christ. God forgives and forgets past sins.

Justification is not brought out in the Bible stories, but is discussed in Paul's writings (Rom. 3:24; Gal. 2:16; Acts 13:39). Paul certainly knew what it meant, for he had been a murderer before he became a Christian. But when he accepted Jesus into his life, Paul was used mightily by God.

100

ADOPTION

A sinner is separated from God. His sin has set a chasm between God and himself. Adam found this when he entered into sin. Before he sinned, Adam was treated as a child of God. He had all of God's favors. But when Adam sinned, he was driven away from God's presence and from God's favors. He was no longer allowed to live as a son.

When a sinner returns to Christ, he is adopted. He returns to that wonderful relationship as a child of God (I John 3: 2). That wonderful relationship could not be held by works. Adam learned that. It can only be held by faith in Jesus Christ (Gal. 3: 26).

The adopted son must remember to live as a son. He must walk as a child of the King.

SANCTIFICATION

Sanctification means to be separated from sin and unto God. When a person becomes a new person in Christ, he is a "sacred vessel" for God's use. He is dedicated to God and His service. He is set apart from other men and their habits and their ways, for God's ways.

The Truth About the Bible

THE BIBLE IS A BOOK. That's what the word means. But it's a special Book. For many years it has been the most widely circulated book in the world. More people have read it than any other book ever written. But most important, more people have based their lives on it than any other book.

What's so special about the Bible? That's what we want to learn.

WHAT THE BIBLE IS

The Bible is the Word of God. In the Bible we learn what God has said and done in the hearts and lives of other people. The Bible is God's message to man, a message of love and hope.

The Bible Is an Inspired Book

To understand the Bible, one must first understand how we received it. One of the great doctrines of the Christian faith has to do with the way we got the Bible. It is called the "inspiration of the Scriptures."

The Bible is an inspired Book. It was inspired by God. That means that the message of the Bible was "breathed" into men by God, so that the written words are God's words, the Word of God to all men.

The Apostle Peter explained inspiration this way, "Holy men of God were moved by the Holy Ghost" (II Peter 1: 21). This explained the kind of men who could write Scripture, "Holy men of God."

Every writer could not qualify. Only those who were truly holy men of God could write Scripture. But even these men could not write Scripture unless they were "moved by the Holy Ghost." It was the movement of the Holy Spirit which brought forth Scripture. But it was done through special men of God.

The message given in II Timothy 3: 16 summarizes the way we received the Bible, "All Scripture is given by inspiration of God."

The Bible Is a Book About God

The Bible tells us about God. It is a Book about the Father, the Son, and the Holy Spirit. It tells about Heaven, and how to get there. It tells about God's people and His plans for His people. It tells how God wants His people to live enroute to Heaven.

102

The Bible also tells about Hell and sin. It warns people who have not given themselves to God, through Christ, about the punishment for sin. It tells about the sad ending of a sinful life in eternal punishment. It warns nations which turn from God, too, telling of their unhappy future without God.

Thus, the Bible is not only a revelation from God, it is a revelation about God. It is God's Word, telling about God and His ways. It reveals or shows God's rules for happy living. It shows how other people of God have lived, too.

WHAT THE BIBLE DOES

Converts the soul (Psalm 19:7)
Makes wise the simple (Psalm 19:7)
Cleans the heart (John 15:3)
Cleans our ways (Psalm 119:9)
Builds faith (Acts 20:32)
Comforts (Psalm 119:82; Rom. 15:4)
Helps us grow in grace (I Pet. 2:2)
Supports life (Deut. 8:3; Matt. 4:4)
Keeps us from the wrong ways (Psalm 17:4)
Sanctifies (John 17:17; Eph. 5:26)
Lightens our way (Psalm 119:105, 130)

BIBLE STORIES THAT TEACH ABOUT THE BIBLE

God gave Moses ten commandments and the Law, v. 3, 83-89
Book of the Law was found, v. 5, 92-99
What's in the Bible, v. 3, 192; v. 4, 192; v. 5, 141, 192
What Bible did people have, v. 5, 98, 99
How Epistles and Revelation were written, v. 9, 182-192

The Truth About the Church

WHAT IS THE CHURCH?

There are more than two hundred different kinds of "churches" or groups of believers in this country. Each has many "churches" in communities across the land.

Often this larger group is called "the church." Thus we have "The Methodist Church," "The Catholic Church," "The Church of Christ," and many others. Some groups, such as Baptists, do not want to be called "the church." They are usually called fellowships, or denominations, or conventions. These groups usually give the local church the authority over itself. The larger organization does not have authority over the churches, as many "church" organizations have.

Each of these larger groups has many "churches" in local communities. The group of believers who meet together in one place are really "the church" in that community, not the building.

But we are talking about something different when we speak of "The Church" in this section. We are talking here about "The Church" as the Bible refers to it. All of the larger groups mentioned above came into being since Jesus and the apostles walked on the earth.

"The Church" is the total group of all believers, no matter what name they may call their national or local group. People who have been saved, who have accepted Christ into their lives and follow Him, are members of this Church.

This is explained in Acts 2:47, where it says, "The Lord added to the church such as should be saved." We come to the Lord first, then are added to His church.

The doctrine of The Church, as it has been interpreted by various people, has meant many things to many people. Bible-believing Christians are united on most of the other doctrines of the faith, but the doctrine of The Church often divides them.

People are often divided, not on the truth that the Bible teaches about The Church, but on the things the Bible does not say. Most division comes from ideas about the way The Church is organized and how it works.

We will not discuss here the issues which divide The Church. Rather, we want to talk about the issues which unite The Church.

104

WHAT IS THE CHURCH LIKE?

The Church Is a Body of Believers, with Christ As Its Head

Christ and His Church are part of the same living movement. Christ is the Head over it. The Church is the hands, feet, and lips for it. The Church serves its Head, doing what the Head plans and wishes.

Christ, as Head of the Church, gives life to it (Ephesians 1:23). He guards and protects His Church (Ephesians 5:23, 24), and helps it stay together and grow (Ephesians 4:14; Col. 2:19).

The Church Is the Bride of Christ

The Bible speaks of The Church as Christ's Bride (II Cor. 11:2; Eph. 5:25-27; Rev. 19:7; 22:17). It talks of Christ as the Bridegroom (John 3:29). This suggests a close relationship of love between Christ and His Church, one that will last forever. Christ and His Church will unite, in the one true love story where it can be said, "they lived happily ever after." This story of love will never end. Christ is even now preparing His mansion in Heaven where His bride will live (John 14:1-3). See also Rev. 21:2.

WHAT IS THE CHURCH TO DO?

The Church Is to Worship God and Honor Him

The Church should try to praise and honor God on earth, thanking God for His goodness, and praising Him for all the wonderful things He has done (Eph. 1:4-6.)

The Church Is to Tell the World About Christ

This was the Great Commission which Jesus gave, to go into all the world with the Gospel so that others might be won to Him (Matt. 28:19, 20; Acts 2; 5:42; 6:5-8; 15:7; Eph. 3:8.)

The Church Is to Help Believers Build Strong Christian Lives

Christ wants strong followers, believers who will not fall away in temptation. He wants men and women of purpose and conviction. See the section on "Building Blocks of Character" to see the qualities He wants in His followers. See also Gal. 5:16-25.

The Truth About Angels

THE BIBLE mentions angels many times. They are spoken of as definite beings, not just mystery characters in stories. Here are some of the Bible teachings about angels.

WHAT THEY ARE LIKE

Angels Are Beings, Created by God

The angels are beings which God has created (Neh. 9:6). They are not the spirits of dead men, nor the elevated spirits of living men. They are specific kinds of beings which God has made as angels (Heb. 12:22, 23; Col. 1:16).

Angels Are Spiritual

Angels do not have bodies like ours, but are spirits (Heb. 1:14; Psalm 104:4). Sometimes in the Bible, angels have appeared in such a way that men could see them. Sometimes they appeared to men in human bodies, which were probably put on them for such an appearance (see Gen. 19; Judges 2:1; 6:11-22; Matt. 1:20; Luke 1:26; John 20:12).

Angels, like all heavenly beings, are neither male nor female. Jesus said that people in Heaven do not marry, but are like the angels in Heaven (Matt. 22:30).

Angels Have Great Power

The Bible tells of several times when angels showed great power. One angel killed a hundred and eighty-five thousand Assyrian soldiers (Isaiah 37:36; II Kings 19). Two angels destroyed Sodom and Gomorrah and the surrounding cities (Gen. 19:13). An angel of God rolled the great stone away from Jesus' tomb on the resurrection morning (Matt. 28:2). In the future, an angel of God will have the power to seize Satan and bind him for a thousand years in a pit.

Angels Have Different Ranks

Not all angels are the same. Michael is mentioned as the archangel, which would mean one of the highest angels (I Thess. 4:16; Jude 9). The angel Gabriel probably has a high rank among the angels, for he had the most exciting work of announcing the births of John the Baptist and

106

Jesus (Luke 1:19, 26). I Peter 3:22 and Colossians 1:16 suggest some different ranks among the heavenly beings.

Angels Form a Great Host of Beings

The Bible tells us that there are many angels. God showed Elisha and a young man an army of angels with horses and chariots of fire (II Kings 6:17).

When Jesus was born in Bethlehem, an angel came to the shepherds to announce His birth. With the angel came "a multitude of the heavenly host, praising God" (Luke 2:13-15). In the Garden of Gethsemane, Jesus told Peter that He could ask His Father to send more than "twelve legions of angels" (Matt. 26:53). That would have been at least seventy-two thousand angels!

WHAT DO ANGELS DO?

They lead sinners to Christians and Christians to sinners to help them
    know Christ (Acts 8:26; 10:3).
They give strength and help to Christians (Matt. 4:11; Luke 22:43).
They protect Christians (Acts 5:19; 12:8-11; 27:23, 24).
They watch over the work of Christians (I Cor. 4:9; 11:10; I Tim.
    5:21).
They guard Christians who die (Luke 16:22; Matt. 24:31)
They will come with Christ at His Second Coming (Matt. 25:31, 32;
    II Thess. 1:7, 8).
They will help to punish the wicked (Matt. 13:39-42).

BIBLE STORIES THAT TEACH ABOUT ANGELS

Many Bible stories have already been mentioned. In addition, see the sacrifice of Isaac, v. 2, 97-103; Jacob's ladder, v. 2, 128-133; the burning bush, v. 3, 30-35; Balaam's donkey, v. 3, 115-120; Gideon's army, v. 3, 114-151; the fiery furnace, v. 5, 129-135.

The Truth About Satan

TO SOME PEOPLE, Satan seems to be a joke. They think of him as a story-book character with horns, red suit, and pitchfork. Of course, the Bible does not paint such a picture of Satan. Instead, it tells a sober story of a real being who has armies of evil beings lined up to fight God and His forces. It tells of a being who would destroy your soul with his, hoping to take you with him into his eternal punishment in hell. Who is Satan? What is he like? Those are questions to be answered here.

WHO IS SATAN?

Satan is a real person, not a story-book character. In the wilderness, when Jesus was tempted, Jesus recognized him as a real person (Matt. 4:1-11). He was someone to be feared and respected.

Satan is an extremely evil person. He is a murderer, a liar, and is even the father of lies (John 8:44). Satan is the "prince of this world," which means a high ruler of all the sin and wickedness of this earth (John 14:30). He presides over the world and its forces of evil.

Satan Is Prince of the Power of the Air

As "prince of the power of the air," Satan has the power to work in people of this world (Eph. 2:2). The power which Satan has is permitted by God. God does not give him the evil power, but permits him to have it and use it. Satan can go no farther than God permits. The story of Job shows this clearly.

Satan Is Ruler of This World

Behind all the sinful activities of the world is a powerful person, planning and moving men to do this sin. This person is Satan. (See II Cor. 4:4; Eph. 2:1, 2; John 12:31; 14:30; 16:11; I John 5:19).

Satan Is Ruler of an Enemy Kingdom

Satan and his forces stand opposed to God and His forces. The great battle of the ages seems quiet to us here on earth because we do not sense it with our five earthly senses. But it is a fierce battle, waged with demons and angels and chariots of fire (II Kings 6:17). Satan is the enemy (I Peter 5:8; Matt. 13:39).

108

WHERE DID SATAN COME FROM?

Satan was once in a high place in the spiritual world. But when he tried to set himself above the rank where God had placed him, making himself equal with God, God put him down (Isaiah 14:12-14). See also John 8:44 and I Timothy 3:6.

HOW DOES SATAN WORK?

He blinds the minds of men, keeping them from seeing the light of the Gospel (II Cor. 4:4.)

He uses fiery darts, or arrows, to hurt his enemies (Eph. 6:16.)

He tries to trick his enemies (Eph. 6:16.)

He helps his enemies get hungry for the things of this world (I Jn. 2:15.)

WHAT WILL HAPPEN TO SATAN?

Satan will be bound by an angel and put into a bottomless pit for a thousand years. During this time he cannot hurt the world. Then he will be let out for a while, but will at last be thrown into a lake of fire, prepared for him and his angels (Matt. 25:41; Rev. 20:1-3; 7-10).

BIBLE STORIES THAT TEACH ABOUT SATAN

Satan tempted Eve, v. 2, 14-21; he tested Job, v. 5, 162-171; and he tempted Jesus, v. 6, 78-85.

The Truth About Last Things

WHAT WILL HAPPEN at the end of time? Does the Bible tell us the strange truth about the future? Not as much as we might like. But it does tell us many things. Here are some important truths which the Bible teaches about the future.

JESUS CHRIST WILL COME BACK TO EARTH AGAIN

This truth is often called "The Second Coming of Christ." The Bible clearly teaches that Christ will return to earth again some day. Here are some things the Bible teaches about it.

Jesus Christ will come back to earth some day in the same way that He left the earth, that is, through the sky (Acts 1:11.)

Jesus Christ will come from Heaven when He returns (I Thess. 4:16, 17.)

The whole world will know of His coming, for it will be like lightning (Matt. 24:27; Luke 21:27.)

He will come back at a time when people least expect Him (Luke 12:40; Acts 1:11.)

His coming will bring great joy to those who are ready (Luke 12:37.)

The time of His coming is a secret. Only God the Father knows when that will be. Not even the angels know (Matt. 24:36, 42, 44.)

When He returns, He will send angels throughout the earth to gather His own (Matt. 24:31.)

PEOPLE WILL BE RAISED FROM THE DEAD

The Bible teaches that in the last time, the bodies of all men will be raised from the dead. In John 5:28, we read, "The hour is coming, in which all that are in the graves shall hear His voice, and shall come forth." As death through sin came by Adam, so resurrection will come by Jesus Christ (I Cor. 15:22).

The Bible does not tell exactly what this resurrection body will be like. But it will probably be like the body Jesus had after He returned from the dead.

The Scripture passage in I Corinthians 15:42-51 tells some facts about the resurrection body. It will not get sick, have pain, or deteriorate

110

(v. 42). It will be a glorious body (v. 43). It will not get tired or weak (v. 43). It will be a spiritual body (v. 44-46). It will be suitable for Heaven (v. 47-49).

JESUS CHRIST WILL JUDGE ALL MEN

Jesus Christ will be the judge of all men. "Every knee will bow before Him and every tongue will confess that He is Lord" (Phil. 2:10-11). He will judge the unbeliever for his eternal destiny and the believer for his works as a believer. The judgment of the unbeliever will determine where he lives for eternity. The judgment of the believer will determine how he lives in Heaven for eternity, for it will decide the position or place he will have in Heaven.

MEN WILL BE PUNISHED OR REWARDED

The Bible teaches that the wicked will be punished (Rom. 2:8, 9; Matt. 13:21; 24:9; Rev. 7:14). They will be sent away from the presence of God and Christ, into eternal punishment in fire (Matt. 25:41, 46; II Thess. 1:7-9).

The believers in Christ, who are called the righteous because they have accepted His righteousness, will be given eternal life. They will never die spiritually (John 11:25, 26; I Tim. 5:6).

A believer, one who follows Christ, will be given a crown of life (James 1:12; Rev. 2:10). He will enter Heaven, his new home, where God lives. There he will never again know tears, sorrow, night, cursing, death, or mourning. These are all passed away (Rev. 21:4). But he will know the happy, endless life of joy with Jesus Christ.

BIBLE STORIES THAT TEACH LAST THINGS

Story of the faithful servants teaches Jesus' second coming, v. 7, 120-125; the locked gate, rich man and Lazarus, laborers in vineyard teach about Heaven, v. 7, 126-129, 148-153, 184-189.

How Can We Teach
These Important Doctrines
To Our Children?

1. Make A Daily Habit of Reading the Bible

The Bible is a Book of doctrines. It teaches us about God, Jesus, the Holy Spirit, and the other important doctrines which make up our faith. By reading the Bible, we help the child know what God says.

2. Help the Child Memorize Bible Verses

Choose important memory verses which teach these doctrines. Make a practice of memorizing at least one or two each week. This will put God's Word at work in the child's heart.

3. Talk About These Important Doctrines

Explain their meaning to the child. If you don't know, then read the pages where it has been explained in this volume. Talk about these things as you go about your activities, as well as in family devotions.

4. Go With Your Child to Church and Sunday School

He will hear preaching and teaching to help him understand these important truths. It's important that you *take* him, not *send* him.

5. Pray That God Will Enlighten Your Understanding

It is God who gives wisdom for us to understand. Of all that we learn, these doctrines, or teachings, are the most important. Remember to ask God for special wisdom to understand them.

Through-the-Bible
Study Guide
and Scripture Index

How to Use These Pages for Bible Study

The following pages may be used effectively in your personal or family Bible study. They will guide you through a storehouse of Bible materials —helping you learn about people, places, customs, periods of history, homes, clothing, and a wealth of other information about the Bible setting. They will lead you to questions which help you apply Bible truth into everyday living. And they will point you to stories which help you and your family re-live the important events of the Bible.

You may use these pages as a simple reference guide. When studying a certain passage of Scripture, look it up in this guide. It will refer you to additional study materials in volumes 2-9.

Or you may use these pages as a CHAIN-REACTION METHOD OF BIBLE STUDY. When you look up a Scripture reference, it will guide you to certain pages of study materials. These will also have references which will guide you into related subjects, and so on.

EX- AMPLE	You are studying the story of Jesus healing the nobleman's son in *John 4:43-54*.
STEP 1	Look up *John 4:43-54* in the following study guide. You will find the following references: *John 4:43-54; John 4:46-54;* and *John 4:52,* all relating to this story.
STEP 2	These references will direct you to the following volume and page numbers: Volume 6, pages 96, 118-121, 122, 144, 145, and Volume 7, pages 38 and 176. You can look up any or all of these in your study.
STEP 3	You choose to look up Volume 6, pages 118-121. There you find the story of Jesus healing the nobleman's son. You find the following facts in the story:

(1) Jesus was at Cana when He healed the boy, (2) the nobleman's home was at Capernaum, (3) the time of the healing was one o'clock in the afternoon.

STEP 4 You choose one or all of these topics to look up.

STEP 4A If you choose to study time, a chart follows, on pages 122 and 123, giving a visual comparison of our time and time in Bible days. It gives references which show what happened at the various hours of the day. You could make a study of these references of the events of the Bible that happened at certain times.

STEP 4B You may choose to study the place where Jesus was when He performed the miracle. You may look up CANA in the topical index. It will refer you to Volume 6, pages 92-95 for another event which took place at Cana, and Volume 6, pages 96, 97 for a map and photo of Cana. These references will give you additional references which you can study, such as Nathanael, whose home town was Cana.

STEP 4C Or you may choose to study the place where the nobleman lived. You may look up CAPERNAUM in the topical index. It will refer you to Volume 6, page 19, where you will learn that this was Jesus' second home town, or to Volume 6, page 96, where you will learn that Jesus visited Capernaum after the wedding feast at Cana. It will also refer you to Volume 6, pages 144 and 145, where you learn about Capernaum itself and will see a map and photo of it.

STEP 4D You may follow the references you find in any or all of the above. The chain reaction will continue as long as you wish to follow it.

The CHAIN-REACTION METHOD OF BIBLE STUDY helps you move along an interesting path which never ends until you want to stop. You follow a sequence of ideas or topics or Scripture references which relate to one another.

124

125

127

132

134

Four Steps
To Better Bible Study

1. Learn What the Bible Says

Try to understand what God is saying in the Bible. What do some of the words actually tell you? What thoughts are communicated?

2. Learn What the Bible Means

When you have discovered what the Bible says, try to understand the meaning. God's actions and negotiations with a Bible-time person established certain timeless truths which were important to people in Bible times and are equally important to people today.

3. Learn What the Bible Means to You

It is not enough to understand the meaning of a timeless truth. That truth has certain meaning to you in your own situation. What is it? What new meaning in life have you gained as a result of this truth?

4. Learn What You Can Do About It

To learn truth is important. But it is the beginning, not the end. God wants us to apply the truth we have learned so that it may find expression in our hands and feet and lips. Truth at work is truth in daily life. But it must be God's truth as found in His Word.

Bible People

Study Guide and Index

Bible People
Study Guide and Index

How to Use These Pages for Bible Study

The Bible people who are mentioned in volumes 2 through 9 are listed on the following pages. With each person you will find the volume and page numbers where important information on this person may be found. You may use this study guide as an index or for the CHAIN REACTION METHOD OF BIBLE STUDY, described on the opening pages of the *Through-the-Bible Study Guide*.

138

SAUL, *cont.*

Evil spirit comes upon him,
Vol. 4, p. 49
David plays for him, Vol. 4, pp. 49-53
Gives David armor to fight giant,
Vol. 4, p. 59
Jealous of David, Vol. 4, pp. 70-74
Tries to kill David, Vol. 4, pp. 88-93
Life spared by David, Vol. 4, pp. 88-93
Visits Witch of Endor,
Vol. 4, pp. 108-112
Dies, Vol. 4, p. 112
Life of, Vol. 4, p. 113
See also, Vol. 4, pp. 12, 41, 54, 55,
101, 140, 177
Vol. 5, pp. 178, 189

SAUL OF TARSUS (*See* Paul)

SCEVA
Seven sons of, Vol. 9, pp. 126-129

SEBA
Noah's descendant, Vol. 2, p. 48

SERUG
Noah's descendant, Vol. 2, p. 49

SETH
Adam's son, Vol. 2, p. 27

SETHUR
One of twelve spies, Vol. 3, p. 109

SHADRACH
Daniel's friend, Vol. 5, pp. 124-126
In fiery furnace, Vol. 5, pp. 129-134

SHALLUM, King of Israel
Vol. 5, pp. 24, 110, 111

SHAMGAR, Judge
Vol. 3, p. 157
Vol. 4, p. 101

SHAMMAH
Son of Jesse, Vol. 3, p. 175
Vol. 4, pp. 45, 95
In Saul's army, Vol. 4, p. 56

SHAMMUA
One of twelve spies, Vol. 3, p. 109

SHAPHAN
The scribe, Vol. 5, pp. 94, 95

SHAPHAT
One of twelve spies, Vol. 3, p. 109

SHEBA, Queen of
Visits Solomon, Vol. 4, pp. 186-189

SHEBAH
Ham's descendant, Vol. 2, p. 48

SHEBAH
Shem's descendant, Vol. 2, p. 49

SHELEPH
Noah's descendant, Vol. 2, p. 49

SHEM
Noah's son, Vol. 2, pp. 36, 45, 49

SHEMEBER, King of Zeboiim
Vol. 2, p. 79

SHEPHATIAH
David's son, Vol. 4, p. 95

SHIMEA
David's son, Vol. 4, p. 95

SHIMEI
Moses' descendant, Vol. 3, p. 29

SHINAB, King of Admah
Vol. 2, p. 79

SHISHAK, King of Egypt
Vol. 5, p. 18

SHOBAB
David's son, Vol. 4, p. 95

SHUAH
Abraham's son, Vol. 2, p. 90

SHUNEM, Woman of
Gives Elisha a room,
Vol. 5, pp. 46-49, 58
Elisha restores her son, Vol. 5, p. 59
See also, Vol. 3, p. 180

SIDON
Noah's descendant, Vol. 2, p. 49

SIHON, King of Amorites
Vol. 3, pp. 115-119

SILAS
Goes with Paul on 2nd missionary
journey, Vol. 9, pp. 94-97
In Philippian jail, Vol. 9, pp. 106-111
In Corinth with Paul,
Vol. 9, pp. 120-124
See also, Vol. 9, pp. 104, 105

SIMEON
Joseph's brother, Vol. 2, pp. 169, 178

SIMEON
Sees Baby Jesus in Temple,
Vol. 6, pp. 40-43

SIMON
A Pharisee, Vol. 6, p. 186
Jesus visits with him,
Vol. 6, pp. 186-189

SIMON, the Sorcerer
Wants to buy gift of Holy Spirit,
Vol. 9, p. 22
See also, Vol. 8, p. 177

SIMON, the Tanner
Vol. 9, pp. 62, 63

SIMON, the Zealot
One of twelve disciples,
Vol. 8, p. 131

SISERA, General
Vol. 3, pp. 137-142

SOLOMON
Anointed king, Vol. 4, p. 18
David's son, Vol. 4, p. 95

SOLOMON, *cont.*
   Prayer for wisdom,
      Vol. 4, pp. 131, 166-169
   Offers 1,000 burnt offerings at Gibeon,
      Vol. 4, p. 166
   Makes offering at Jerusalem,
      Vol. 4, p. 169
   Was he wise? Vol. 4, pp. 170, 171
   His wise judgment, Vol. 4, pp. 172-176
   Builds the Temple,
      Vol. 4, pp. 157, 179-183, 184, 185,
         190, 191
      Vol. 6, p. 103
   Has great riches, Vol. 4, pp. 186-189
   Queen of Sheba visits,
      Vol. 4, pp. 186-189
   See also, Vol. 4, p. 177
         Vol. 5, pp. 45, 179
         Vol. 6, p. 59
SOSTHENES
   Vol. 9, pp. 122-124
STEPHEN
   Deacon, Vol. 8, pp. 189, 190
   Stoned, Vol. 9, pp. 8-12
   Who was he? Vol. 9, p. 13
   See also, Vol. 9, p. 98
SYRIA, King of
   Vol. 5, p. 54
SYRIANS
   Vol. 5, p. 59

TABITHA (*See* Dorcas)
TAMAR
   David's daughter, Vol. 4, p. 141
TAMAR
   Judah's daughter-in-law, Vol. 4, p. 94
TARSHISH
   Noah's descendant, Vol. 2, p. 48
TERAH
   Abraham's father, Vol. 2, pp. 49, 90
   Moves from Ur, Vol. 2, pp. 56-60
TERTULLUS
   Vol. 9, pp. 146-149
THADDAEUS
   One of twelve disciples,
      Vol. 8, p. 131
THOMAS
   One of twelve disciples,
      Vol. 8, p. 131
   Doubts, Vol. 8, pp. 132-137
   See also, Vol. 8, p. 143
TIDAL, King of Goiim
   Vol. 2, p. 79
TIGLATH-PILESER
   Vol. 5, p. 119

TIMON
   Deacon, Vol. 8, p. 189
TIMOTHY
   Son of Eunice, Vol. 9, p. 95
   Goes with Paul,
      Vol. 9, pp. 95, 96
   See also, Vol. 9, p. 120
TIRAS
   Noah's descendant, Vol. 2, p. 48
TITUS JUSTUS
   Vol. 9, p. 122
TOGARMAH
   Noah's descendant, Vol. 2, p. 48
TOLA
   Vol. 3, p. 157
TUBAL
   Noah's descendant, Vol. 2, p. 48
TUBAL-CAIN
   Adam's descendant, Vol. 2, p. 27

URIAH
   Sent by David to die in battle,
      Vol. 4, p. 135
UZ
   Noah's descendant, Vol. 2, p. 49
UZAL
   Noah's descendant, Vol. 2, p. 49
UZZAH
   Dies when he touches ark,
      Vol. 4, pp. 123, 124
UZZIAH, King of Judah
   Becomes a leper, Vol. 5, pp. 60-63
   His life, Vol. 5, pp. 64, 65
   See also, Vol. 5, pp. 25, 110, 111
UZZIEL
   Moses' uncle, Vol. 3, p. 29

WISE MEN
   Follow the star, Vol. 6, pp. 47-51
   Bring gifts to Jesus,
      Vol. 6, pp. 47-53

ZACCHAEUS
   A tax collector, Vol. 8, p. 14
   Climbs a tree to see Jesus,
      Vol. 8, pp. 14-17
ZACHARIAS
   Angel appears to him,
      Vol. 3, p. 180
      Vol. 6, pp. 9-11
ZALMUNNA
   Vol. 3, p. 151
   Vol. 7, p. 69
ZAREPHATH, Widow of
   Elijah helps, Vol. 5, pp. 26-31

What We Learn
From Bible People

1. Examples of Greatness

Great men of the Bible teach us lessons of greatness. We see God at work in their lives. We watch their lives respond to His touch. We learn by their example as they lived great lives for God.

2. Lessons of Warning

There were others who did not achieve greatness. God gave them opportunities, but they wasted their gifts. It is a sad, but important, lesson to watch the lives of those who "went the other way," the way that led from God. These can be lessons of warning for us to heed.

3. Words of Wisdom

The words that great men of God spoke can shape our lives in wonderful ways. Men who walked with God left words of wisdom for us to learn and apply. These words teach us important lessons we should never forget. Many of them echo the truths which these men learned from God.

Topical

Study Guide and Index

Topical
Study Guide and Index

How to Use These Pages for Bible Study

The important topics which are covered in volumes 2 through 9 are listed in the following pages. This study guide may be used as an index, or you may wish to use it for the CHAIN-REACTION METHOD OF BIBLE STUDY, described on the opening pages of the *Through-the Bible Study Guide*.

166

174

176

177

187

188

192